René-Antoine Houasse, *Morpheus Awakens as Iris Draws Near,* 1690, Palace of Versailles

BULFINCH ILLUSTRATED MYTHOLOGY

KONECKY&KONECKY

Konecky & Konecky
72 Ayers Point Rd.
Old Saybrook, CT 06475

ISBN: 978-1-56852-814-4

Reproductions of works of art in this book obtained
from WIkimedia Commons.

Please visit us on the web at www.koneckyandkonecky.com

Printed in China

CONTENTS

CHAPTER I: Introduction: Greek and Roman Gods and Goddesses. 1

CHAPTER II: Creation. Deluge. Prometheus. Pandora 12

CHAPTER III: Io and Callisto. Diana and Actaeon. The Story of Phaeton 22

CHAPTER IV: Midas. Baucis and Philemon. Pluto and Proserpine 31

CHAPTER V: Pygmalion. Venus and Adonis. Apollo and Hyacinthus. Ceyx and Halcyone. 39

CHAPTER VI: Vertumnus and Pomona. Cupid and Psyche 45

CHAPTER VII: Cadmus. The Myrmidons 55

CHAPTER VIII: Nisus and Scylla. Echo and Narcissus. Hero and Leander 59

CHAPTER IX: Minerva and Arachne. Niobe. The Story of Perseus 63

CHAPTER X: Monsters. Giants. Sphinx. Pegasus and the Chimaera. Centaurs 71

CHAPTER XI: The Golden Fleece. Medea. The Calydonian Hunt 75

CHAPTER XII: The Labors of Hercules 84

CHAPTER XIII: Theseus. Daedalus. Castor and Pollux 89

CHAPTER XIV: Bacchus. Ariadne 94

CHAPTER XV: Alcestis. Antigone. Penelope 99

CHAPTER XVI: Orpheus and Eurydice. Aristaeus 102

CHAPTER XVII: Endymion. Orion. Aurora and Tithonus. Acis and Galatea 106

CHAPTER XVIII: The Trojan War 109

CHAPTER XIX: The Fall of Troy. Return of the Greeks. Orestes and Electra 119

CHAPTER XX: The Odyssey 125

Gerard Lairesse, *Apollo and Aurora,* oil on canvas, Metropolitan Museum of Art, New York

CHAPTER I: INTRODUCTION.

The literature of our time, as of all the centuries of Christendom, is full of allusions to the gods and goddesses of the Greeks and Romans. The object of this book is to teach readers who are not yet familiar with the writers of Greece and Rome, enough of the stories which form what is called their mythology, to make those allusions intelligible which one meets every day, even in the authors of our own time. The Greeks and Romans both belong to the same race or stock. So far as we know its history, the Greeks and Romans descended from the tribes that emigrated from the high tablelands of Northern India. Other tribes emigrated in different directions from the same center, so that traces of the Indo-European language are found in the islands of the Pacific Ocean. The people of this race, who moved westward, seemed to have had a special fondness for nature, and a willingness to personify the powers of nature. They were glad to live in the open air, and they specially encouraged the virtues which an open-air people prize. Thus no Roman was thought manly who could not swim, and every Greek exercised in the athletic sports of the palaestra. The Romans and Grecian and German divisions of this great race are those with which we have most to do in history and in literature. Our own English language is made up of the dialects of different tribes, many of whom agreed in their use of words that they had derived from our Aryan ancestry. Thus our substantive verb I AM appears in Sanskrit as ESMI, and m for ME (MOI), or the first person singular, is found in all the verbal inflections. The Greek form of the same verb was ESMI, which became ASMI, and in Latin the first and last vowels have disappeared, the verb is SUM. Similar relationships are traced in the numerals, and throughout all the languages of these nations. The Romans, like the Etruscans who came before them, were neither poetical nor imaginative in temperament. Their activity ran in practical directions. They therefore invented few, if any stories, of the gods whom they worshipped with fixed rites. Mr. Macaulay speaks of these gods as "the sober abstractions of the Roman pantheon." We owe most of the stories of the ancient mythology to the wit and fancy of the Greeks, more playful and imaginative, who seized from Egypt and from the East such legends as pleased them, and adapted them in their own way. It often happens that such stories, resembling each other in their foundation, are found in the Greek and Roman authors in several different forms.

To understand these stories, we will here first acquaint ourselves with the ideas of the structure of the universe, which the poets and others held, and which will form the scenery, so to speak, of the narratives. The Greek poets believed the earth to be flat and circular, their own country occupying the middle of it, the central point being either Mount Olympus, the abode of the gods, or Delphi, so famous for its oracle. The circular disk of the earth was crossed from west to east, and divided into two equal parts by the Sea, as they called the Mediterranean, and its continuation the Euxine. Around the earth flowed the river Ocean, its course being from south to north on the western side of the earth, and in a contrary direction on the eastern side. It flowed in a steady, equable current, unvexed by storm or tempest. The sea, and all the rivers on earth, received their waters from it. The northern portion of the earth was supposed to be inhabited by a happy race named the Hyperboreans (this word means "who live beyond the north" from the word "hyper," beyond, and Boreas, the north wind), dwelling in everlasting bliss and spring beyond the lofty mountains whose caverns were supposed to send forth the piercing blasts of the north wind, which chilled the people of Hellas (Greece). Their country was inaccessible by land or sea. They lived exempt from disease or old age, from toils and warfare. On the south side of the earth, close to the stream of Ocean, dwelt a people happy and virtuous as the Hyperboreans. They were named the Aethiopians. The gods favored them so highly that they were wont to leave at times their Olympian abodes, and go to share their sacrifices and banquets. On the western margin of the earth, by the stream of Ocean, lay a happy place named the Elysian Plain, whither mortals favored by the gods were transported without tasting of death, to enjoy an immortality of bliss. This happy region was also called the "fortunate fields," and the "Isles of the Blessed." We thus see that the Greeks of the early ages knew little of any real people except those to the east and south of their own country, or near the coast of the Mediterranean. Their imagination meantime peopled the western portion of this sea with giants, monsters, and enchantresses; while they placed around the disk of the earth, which they probably regarded as of no great width, nations enjoying the peculiar favor of the gods, and blessed with happiness and longevity. The Dawn, the Sun, and the Moon were supposed to rise out of the Ocean, on the eastern side, and to drive through the air, giving light to gods and men. The stars also, except those forming Charles' Wain or Bear, and others near them, rose out of and sank into the stream of Ocean. There the sun god embarked in a winged boat, which conveyed him round by the northern part of the earth, back to his place of rising in the east.

The abode of the gods was on the summit of Mount Olympus, in Thessaly. A gate of clouds, kept by the goddesses named the Seasons, opened to permit the passage of the Celestials to earth, and to receive them on their return. The gods had their separate dwellings; but all, when summoned, repaired to the palace of Jupiter (or Zeus: the relation of these names to each other will be explained below), as did also those deities whose usual abode was the earth, the waters, or the underworld. It was also in the great hall of the palace of the Olympian king that the gods feasted each day on ambrosia and nectar, their food and drink, the latter being handed round by the lovely goddess Hebe. Here they conversed of the affairs of heaven and earth; and as they quaffed their nectar, Apollo, the god of music, delighted

Giovanni Bellini, *The Feast of the Gods,* 1514, oil on canvas, National Gallery of Art, Washington, DC

them with the tones of his lyre, to which the muses sang in responsive strains. When the sun was set, the gods retired to sleep in their respective dwellings. The following lines from the Odyssey will show how Homer conceived of Olympus:

> *So saying, Minerva, goddess azure-eyed,*
> *Rose to Olympus, the reputed seat*
> *Eternal of the gods, which never storms*
> *Disturb, rains drench, or snow invades, but calm*
> *The expanse and cloudless shines with purest day.*
> *Tis here the inhabitants divine rejoice Forever.*

Such were the abodes of the gods as the Greeks conceived them. The Romans, before they knew the Greek poetry, seem to have had no definite imagination of such an assembly of gods. But the Roman and Etruscan races were by no means irreligious. They venerated their departed ancestors, and in each family the worship of these ancestors was an important duty. The images of the ancestors were kept in a sacred place, each family observed, at fixed times, memorial rites in their honor, and for these and other religious observances the family hearth was consecrated. The earliest rites of Roman worship are supposed to be connected with such family devotions. As the Greeks and Romans became acquainted with other nations, they imported their habits of worship, even in early times. It will be remembered that as late as St. Paul's time, he found an altar at Athens "to an unknown god." Greeks and Romans alike were willing to receive from other nations the legends regarding their gods, and to incorporate them as well as they could with their own. It is thus that in the poetical mythology of those nations, which we are now to study, we frequently find a Latin and a Greek name for one imagined divinity. Thus Zeus, of the Greeks, becomes in Latin Jupiter with the addition of the word pater (a father). Hephaistos of the Greeks appears as "Vulcan" of the Latins, "Ares" of the Greeks is "Mars" of the Latins, "Poseidon" of the Greeks is "Neptune" of the Latins, "Aphrodite" of the Greeks is "Venus" of the Latins. This variation is not to be confounded with a mere translation, as where "Paulos" of the Greek becomes "Paul" in Latin, or "Odysseus" becomes "Ulysses," or as when "Pierre" of the French becomes "Peter" in English. What really happened was, that as the Romans, more cultivated than their fathers, found in Greek literature a god of fire and smithery, they transferred his name "Hephaistos" to their own old god "Vulcan," who had the same duties, and thereafter in their literature the Latin name was used for the stories of Greek and Latin origin. As the English literature came into being largely on French and Latin models, and as French is but a degraded Latin and retains Latin roots largely, in our older English poets the Latin forms of these names are generally used. In our own generation, with the precision now so much courted, a fashion has come in, of designating Mars by his Greek name of "Ares," Venus by her name of "Aphrodite," and so on. But in this book, as our object is to make familiar the stores of general English literature which refer to such subjects, we shall retain, in general, the Latin names, only calling the attention of the reader to the Greek names, as they appear in Greek authors. The real monarch of the heavens in the mythology of both Greece and Rome is Jupiter (Zeus-pater, father-Jove) (Jove appears to be a word derived from the same root as Zeus, and it appears

in the root dev of the Sanskrit, where devas are gods of different forms. Our English word devil probably comes from the French diable, Italian diavolo, Latin diabolus, one who makes division—literally one who separates balls, or throws balls about—instead of throwing them frankly and truly at the batsman. It is not to be traced to the Sanskrit deva.)

In the mythological system we are tracing Zeus is himself the father of many of the gods and goddesses. He is the father of Vulcan, of Venus, of Minerva, of Apollo, Diana (in Greek Artemis), and of Mercury (in Greek Hermes), who are ranked among the twelve superior gods, and of many inferior deities.

But Jupiter himself is not the original deity in these systems. He is the son of Saturn, as in the Greek Zeus is the son of Kronos. Still the inevitable question would occur where did Saturnus or Kronos come from. And, in forms and statements more and more vague, the answer was that he was born from Uranus or Ouranos, which is the name of the Heaven over all which seemed to embrace all things. The Greek name of Saturn was spelled Kronos. The Greek name of Time was spelled Chronos. A similarity between the two was imagined. And the whole statement, when reduced to rationalistic language, would be that from Uranus, the infinite, was born Chronos, Time,—that from Time, Zeus or Jupiter was born, and that he is the only child of Time who has complete sway over mortals and immortals. "The will of Jove I own, Who mortals and immortals rules alone" (Homer). Jupiter was son of Saturn (Kronos) and Ops (Rhea in Greek, sometimes confounded with the Phrygian Cybele). Saturn and Rhea were of the race of Titans, who were the children of Earth and Heaven, which sprang from Chaos, of which we shall give a further account in our next chapter. In allusion to the dethronement of Ouranos by Kronos, and of Kronos or Saturn by Zeus or Jupiter, Prometheus says in Aeschylus's tragedy:

You may deem
Its towers impregnable; but have I not
Already seen two monarchs hurled from them.

There is another cosmogony, or account of the creation, according to which Earth, Erebus, and Love were the first of beings. Love (Eros) issued from the egg of Night, which floated on Chaos. By his arrows and torch he pierced and vivified all things, producing life and joy.

Saturn and Rhea were not the only Titans. There were others, whose names were Oceanus, Hyperion, Iapetus, and Ophion, males; and Themis, Mnemosyne, Eurynome, females. They are spoken of as the elder gods, whose dominion was afterwards transferred to others. Saturn yielded to Jupiter, Oceanus to Neptune, Hyperion to Apollo. Hyperion was the father of the Sun, Moon, and Dawn. He is therefore the original sun god and is painted with the splendor and beauty that were afterwards bestowed on Apollo. Ophion and Eurynome ruled over Olympus until Saturn and Rhea dethroned them.

The representations given of Saturn are not very consistent, for on the one hand his reign is said to have been the golden age of innocence and purity, and on the other he is described as a monster who devoured his own children. (This inconsistency arises from considering the Saturn of the Romans the same with the Grecian deity Chronos, which, as it brings an end to all things which have had a beginning, may be said to devour its own offspring.) Jupiter, however, escaped this fate, and when grown up espoused Metis (Prudence), who administered a draught to Saturn which caused him to disgorge his children. Jupiter, with his brothers and sisters, now rebelled against their father Saturn, and his brothers the Titans, vanquishing them. They imprisoned some of them in Tartarus and inflicted other penalties on others. Atlas was condemned to bear up the heavens on his shoulders. On the dethronement of Saturn, Jupiter with his brothers Neptune and Pluto (Hades) divided his dominions. Jupiter's portion was the heavens, Neptune's the ocean, and Pluto's the realms of the dead. Earth and Olympus were common property. Jupiter was king of gods and men. The thunderbolt was his weapon, and he bore a shield called Aegis, made for him by Vulcan. The eagle was

Peter Paul Rubens, *Saturn Devouring One of His Sons,* 1636, oil on canvas, Prado, Madrid

Sandro Botticelli, *The Birth of Venus,* **c. 1480, Tempera on panel, Uffizi Gallery, Florence**

his favorite bird and bore his thunderbolts. Juno (Hera) was the wife of Jupiter, and queen of the gods. Iris, the goddess of the rainbow, was her attendant and messenger. The peacock was her favorite bird. Vulcan, the celestial artist, was the son of Jupiter and Juno. He was born lame, and his mother was so displeased at the sight of him that she flung him out of heaven. Other accounts say that Jupiter kicked him out for taking part with his mother in a quarrel that occurred between them. Vulcan's lameness, according to this account, was the consequence of his fall. He was a whole day falling, and at last alighted in the island of Lemnos, which was thenceforth sacred to him.

Mars, the god of war, was the son of Jupiter and Juno. Phoebus Apollo (this is a Greek name of a Greek divinity, who seems to have had no Roman resemblance), the god of archery, prophecy, and music, was the son of Jupiter and Latona, and brother of Diana (Artemis). He was god of the sun, as Diana, his sister, was the goddess of the moon. Venus, the goddess of love and beauty, was the daughter of Jupiter and Dione. Others say that Venus sprang from the foam of the sea. The zephyr wafted her along the waves to the Isle of Cyprus, where she was received and attired by the Seasons, and then led to the assembly of the gods. All were charmed with her beauty, and each one demanded her for his wife. Jupiter gave her to Vulcan, in gratitude for the service he had rendered in forging thunderbolts. So the most beautiful of the goddesses became the wife of the most ill favored of the gods. Venus possessed an embroidered girdle called the Cestus, which had the power

Sandro Botticelli, *Venus and Mars,* 1483, tempera on panel, National Gallery, London

of inspiring love. Her favorite birds were swans and doves, and the plants sacred to her were the rose and the myrtle. Cupid (Eros), the god of love, was the son of Venus. He was her constant companion; and, armed with bow and arrows, he shot the darts of desire into the bosoms of both gods and men. There was a deity named Anteros, who was sometimes represented as the avenger of slighted love, and sometimes as the symbol of reciprocal affection. The following legend is told of him: Venus, complaining to Themis that her son Eros continued always a child, was told by her that it was because he was solitary, and that if he had a brother he would grow apace. Anteros was soon afterwards born, and Eros immediately was seen to increase rapidly in size and strength.

Minerva (Pallas Athena), the goddess of wisdom, was the offspring of Jupiter, without a mother. She sprang from his head, completely armed. Her favorite bird was the owl, and the plant sacred to her the olive.

Mercury was the son of Jupiter and Maia. He presided over commerce, wrestling and other gymnastic exercises; even over thieving, and everything, in short, which required skill and dexterity. He was the messenger of Jupiter and wore a winged cap and winged shoes. He bore in his hand a rod entwined with two serpents, called the Caduceus. Mercury is said to have invented the lyre. Four hours after his birth he found the shell of a tortoise, made holes in the opposite edges of it, and drew cords of linen through them, and the instrument was complete (From this origin of the instrument, the word "shell" is often used as synonymous with "lyre," and figuratively for music and poetry.) The cords were nine, in honor of the nine Muses. Mercury gave the lyre to Apollo and received from him in exchange the caduceus.

Ceres (Demeter) was the daughter of Saturn and Rhea. She had a daughter named Proserpine (Persephone), who became the wife of Pluto and queen of the realms of the dead. Ceres presided over agriculture.

Bacchus (Dionysus), the god of wine, was the son of Jupiter and Semele. He represents not only the intoxicating power of wine, but its social and beneficent influences likewise, so that he is viewed as the promoter of civilization, and a lawgiver and lover of peace.

The muses were the daughters of Jupiter and Mnemosyne (Memory). They presided over song and prompted the memory. They were nine in number, to each of whom was assigned the presidency over some particular department of literature, art, or science. Calliope was the muse of epic poetry, Clio of history, Euterpe of lyric poetry, Melpomene of tragedy, Terpischore of choral dance and song, Erato of love-poetry, Polyhymnia of sacred poetry, Urania of astronomy, Thalia of comedy.

The Fates were also three: Clotho, Lachesis, and Atropos. Their office was to spin the thread of human destiny, and they were armed with shears, with which they cut it off when they pleased. They were the daughters of Themis (Law), who sits by Jove on his throne to give him counsel.

The Erinnyes, or Furies, were three goddesses who punished crimes by their secret stings. The heads of the Furies were wreathed with serpents, and their whole appearance was terrific and appalling. Their names were Alecto, Tisiphone, and Megaera. They were also called Eumenides. Nemesis was also an avenging goddess. She represents the righteous anger of the gods, particularly towards the proud and insolent.

Pan (the name Pan means everything, and he is sometimes spoken of as the god of all nature) was the god of flocks and shepherds. His favorite residence, as the Greeks describe him, was in Arcadia. The Satyrs were deities of the woods and fields. They were conceived to be covered with bristly hair, their heads decorated with short, sprouting horns, and their feet like goats' feet. Momus was the god of laughter, and Plutus the god of wealth.

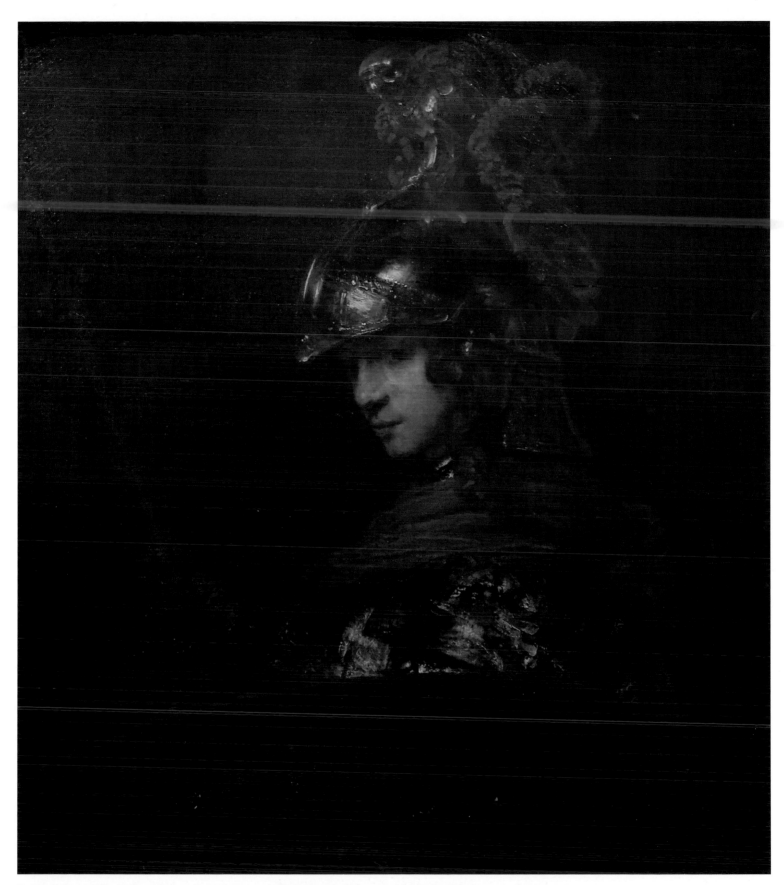

Rembrandt von Rijn, *Pallas Athena,* **oil on canvas, c. 1655, Gulbenkian Museum, Lisbon, Portugal** (Photograph © Yelkrokoyade)

Bernardo Strozzi, *The Three Fates,* mid-seventeenth century

ROMAN DIVINITIES

The preceding are Grecian divinities, though received also by the Romans. Those that follow are peculiar to Roman mythology. Saturn was an ancient Italian deity. The Roman poets tried to identify him with the Grecian god Kronos and fabled that after his dethronement by Jupiter, he fled to Italy, where he reigned during what was called the Golden Age. In memory of his beneficent dominion, the feast of Saturnalia was held every year in the winter season. Then all public business was suspended, declarations of war and criminal executions were postponed, friends made presents to one another, and the slaves were indulged with great liberties. A feast was given them at which they sat at table, while their masters served them, to show the natural equality of men, and that all things belonged equally to all, in the reign of Saturn.

Faunus (there was also a goddess called Fauna, or Bona Dea), the grandson of Saturn, was worshipped as the god of fields and shepherds, and also as a prophetic god. His name in the plural, Fauns, expressed a class of gamesome deities, like the Satyrs of the Greeks.

Quirinus was a war god, said to be none other than Romulus the founder of Rome, exalted after his death to a place among the gods. Bellona, a war goddess. Terminus, the god of landmarks. His statue was a rude stone or post, set in the ground to mark the boundaries of fields. Pales, the goddess presiding over cattle and pastures. Pomona presided over fruit trees. Flora, the goddess of flowers. Lucina, the goddess of childbirth. Vesta (the Hestia of the Greeks) was a deity presiding over the public and private hearth. A sacred fire, tended by six virgin priestesses called Vestals, flamed in her temple. As the safety of the city was held to be connected with its conservation, the neglect of the virgins, if they let it go out, was severely punished, and the fire was rekindled from the rays of the sun.

Liber is another Latin name of Bacchus; and Mulciber of Vulcan. Janus was the porter of heaven. He opens the year, the first month being named after him. He is the guardian deity of gates, on which account he is commonly represented with two heads, because every door looks two ways. His temples at Rome were numerous. In wartime the gates of the principal one were always open. In peace they were closed; but they were shut only once between the reign of Numa and that of Augustus.

The Penates were the gods who were supposed to attend to the welfare and prosperity of the family. Their name is derived from Penus, the pantry, which was sacred to them. Every master of a family was the priest to the Penates of his own house. The Lares, or Lars, were also household gods, but differed from the Penates in being regarded as the deified spirits of mortals. The family Lars were held to be the souls of the ancestors, who watched over and protected their descendants. The words Lemur and Larva more nearly correspond to our word Ghost. The Romans believed that every man had his Genius, and every woman her Juno; that is, a spirit who had given them being, and was regarded as a protector through life. On birthdays men made offerings to their Genius, women to their Juno.

N.B. It is to be observed that in proper names the final e and es are to be sounded. Thus Cybele and Penates are words of three syllables. But Proserpine and Thebes have been so long used as English words, that they may be regarded as exceptions, to be pronounced as if English. The poets sometimes pronounce Hecate as a dissyllable.

CHAPTER II: CREATION. DELUGE. PROMETHEUS. PANDORA.

The Roman poet Ovid gives us a connected narrative of creation. Before the earth and sea and the all-covering heaven, one aspect, which we call Chaos, covered all the face of Nature, a rough heap of inert weight and discordant beginnings of things clashing together. As yet no sun gave light to the world, nor did the moon renew her slender horn month by month, neither did the earth hang in the surrounding air, poised by its own weight, nor did the sea stretch its long arms around the earth. Wherever there was earth, there was also sea and air. So the earth was not solid nor was the water fluid, neither was the air transparent. God and Nature at last interposed and put an end to this discord, separating earth from sea, and heaven from both. The fiery part, being the lightest, sprang up and formed the skies; the air was next in weight and place. The earth, being heavier, sank below, and the water took the lowest place and buoyed up the earth. Here some god, no man knows whom, arranged and divided the land. He placed the rivers and bays, raised mountains and dug out valleys and distributed woods, fountains, fertile fields and stony plains. Now that the air was clear, the stars shone out, the fishes swam the sea and birds flew in the air, while the four-footed beasts roamed around the earth. But a nobler animal was needed, and man was made in the image of the gods with an upright stature [The two Greek words for man have the root "an", up], so that while all other animals turn their faces downward and look to the earth, he raises his face to heaven and gazes on the stars. To Prometheus the Titan and to his brother Epimetheus was committed the task of making man and all other animals and of endowing them with all needful faculties. This Epimetheus did, and his brother overlooked the work. Epimetheus then gave to the different animals their several gifts of courage, strength, swiftness and sagacity. He gave wings to one, claws to another, a shell covering to the third. Man, superior to all other animals, came last. But for man Epimetheus had nothing; he had bestowed all his gifts elsewhere. He came to his brother for help, and Prometheus, with the aid of Minerva, went up to heaven, lighted his torch at the chariot of the sun, and brought down fire to man. With this, man was more than equal to all other animals. Fire enabled him to make weapons to subdue wild beasts, tools with which to till the earth. With fire he warmed his dwelling and bid defiance to the cold. Woman was not yet made. The story is, that Jupiter made her and sent her to Prometheus and his brother, to punish them for their presumption in stealing fire from heaven; and man, for accepting the gift. The first woman was named Pandora. She was made in heaven, every god contributing something to perfect her. Venus gave her beauty, Mercury persuasion, Apollo music. Thus equipped, she was conveyed to earth, and presented to Epimetheus, who gladly accepted her, though cautioned by his brother to beware of Jupiter and his gifts. Epimetheus had in his house a jar, in which were kept certain noxious articles, for which, in fitting man for his new abode, he had had no occasion. Pandora was seized with an eager curiosity to know what this jar contained; and one day she slipped off the cover and looked in. Forthwith there escaped a multitude of plagues for hapless man—such as gout, rheumatism, and colic for his body, and envy, spite, and revenge for his mind—and scattered themselves far and wide. Pandora hastened to replace the lid; but, alas! The whole contents of the jar had escaped, one thing only excepted, which lay at the bottom, and that was HOPE. So we see at this day, whatever evils are abroad, hope never entirely leaves us; and while we have that, no amount of other ills can make us completely wretched. Another story is, that Pandora was sent in good faith, by Jupiter, to bless man; that she was furnished with a box, containing her marriage presents, into which every god had put some blessing. She opened the box incautiously, and the blessings all escaped, Hope only excepted. This story seems more consistent than the former; for how could Hope, so precious a jewel as it is, have been kept in a jar full of all manner of evils?

The world being thus furnished with inhabitants, the first age was an age of innocence and happiness, called the Golden Age. Truth and right prevailed, though not enforced by law, nor was there any magistrate to threaten or punish. The forest had not yet been robbed of its trees to furnish timbers for vessels, nor had men built fortifications round their towns. There were no such things as swords, spears, or helmets. The earth brought forth all things necessary for man, without his labor in plowing or sowing. Perpetual spring reigned, flowers sprang up without seed, the rivers flowed with milk and wine, and yellow honey distilled from the oaks.

But when good Saturn, banished from above,
Was driven to hell, the world was under Jove.
Succeeding times a Silver Age behold,
Excelling brass, but more excelled by gold.
Then summer, autumn, winter did appear,
And spring was but a season of the year.
The sun his annual course obliquely made,
Good days contracted and enlarged the bad,

John William Waterhouse, *Pandora,* 1896, oil on canvas, Private collection

Then air, with sultry heats, began to glow;
The wings of winds were clogged with ice and snow
And shivering mortals into houses driven,
Sought shelter from the inclemency of heaven.
Those houses then were caves, or homely sheds;
With twining osiers fenced; and moss their beds.
Then plows, for seed, the fruitful furrows broke,
And oxen labored first beneath the yoke.
To this came next in course the Brazen Age:
A warlike offspring, prompt to bloody rage,
Not impious yet! . . . . . Hard Steel succeeded then;
And stubborn as the metal were the men."

(Ovid's *Metamorphoses*, Book I. Dryden's Translation.)

Crime burst in like a flood; modesty, truth, and honor fled. In their places came fraud and cunning, violence, and the wicked love of gain. Then seamen spread sails to the wind, and the trees were torn from the mountains to serve for keels to ships and vex the face of ocean. The earth, which until now had been cultivated in common, began to be divided off into possessions. Men were not satisfied with what the surface produced, but must dig into its bowels, and draw forth from thence the ores of metals. Mischievous iron, and more mischievous gold, were produced. War sprang up, using both as weapons; the guest was not safe in his friend's house; and sons-in-law and fathers-in-law, brothers and sisters, husbands and wives, could not trust one another. Sons wished their fathers dead, that they might come to the inheritance; family love lay prostrate. The earth was wet with slaughter, and the gods abandoned it, one by one, until Astraea (the goddess of innocence and purity) alone was left. After leaving earth, she was placed among the stars, where she became the constellation Virgo. Themis (Justice) was the mother of Astraea. She is represented as holding aloft a pair of scales, in which she weighs the claims of opposing parties. It was a favorite idea of the old poets, that these goddesses would one day return, and bring back the Golden Age.

Jupiter, seeing this state of things, burned with anger. He summoned the gods to council. They obeyed the call and took the road to the palace of heaven. The road, which any one may see in a clear night, stretches across the face of the sky and is called the Milky Way. Along the road stand the palaces of the illustrious gods; the common people of the skies live apart, on either side. Jupiter addressed the assembly. He set forth the frightful condition of things on the earth, and closed by announcing his intention to destroy the whole of its inhabitants, and provide a new race, unlike the first, who would be more worthy of life, and much better worshippers of the gods. So saying he took a thunderbolt, and was about to launch it at the world, and destroy it by burning it; but recollecting the danger that such a conflagration might set heaven itself on fire, he changed his plan, and resolved to drown the world. Aquilo, the north wind, which scatters the clouds, was chained up; Notus, the south, was sent out, and soon covered all the face of heaven with a cloak of pitchy darkness. The clouds, driven together, resound with a crash; torrents of rain fall; the crops are laid low; the year's labor of the husbandman perishes in an hour. Jupiter, not satisfied with his own waters, calls on his brother Neptune to aid him with his. He lets loose the rivers, and pours them over the land. At the same time, he heaves the land with an earthquake, and brings in the reflux of the ocean over the shores. Flocks, herds, men, and houses are swept away, and temples, with their sacred enclosures, profaned. If any edifice remained standing, it was overwhelmed, and its turrets lay hid beneath the waves. Now all was sea; sea without shore. Here and there some one remained on a projecting hilltop, and a few, in boats, pulled the oar where they had lately driven the plow. The fishes swim among the treetops; the anchor is let down into a garden. Where the graceful lambs played but now, unwieldy sea calves gambol. The wolf swims among the sheep; the yellow lions and tigers struggle in the water. The strength of the wild boar serves him not, nor his swiftness the stag. The birds fall with weary wing into the water, having found no land for a resting place. Those living beings that the water spared fell a prey to hunger. Parnassus alone, of all the mountains, overtopped the waves; and there Deucalion and his wife Pyrrha, of the race of Prometheus, found refuge—he a just man, and she a faithful worshipper of the gods. Jupiter, when he saw none left alive but this pair, and remembered their harmless lives and pious demeanor, ordered the north winds to drive away the clouds, and disclose the skies to earth, and earth to the skies. Neptune also directed Triton to blow on his shell and sound a retreat to the waters. The waters obeyed, and the sea returned to its shores, and the rivers to their channels. Then Deucalion thus addressed Pyrrha: "O wife, only surviving woman, joined to me first by the ties of kindred and marriage, and now by a common danger, would that we possessed the power of our ancestor Prometheus, and could renew the race as he at first made it! But as we cannot, let us seek yonder temple, and inquire of the gods what remains for us to do." They entered the temple, deformed as it was with slime, and approached the altar, where no fire burned. There they fell prostrate on the earth, and prayed the goddess to inform them how they might retrieve their miserable affairs. The oracle answered, "Depart from the temple with head veiled and garments unbound, and cast behind you the bones of your mother." They heard the words with astonishment. Pyrrha first broke silence: "We cannot obey; we dare not profane the remains of our parents." They sought the thickest shades of the wood, and revolved the oracle in their minds. At length Deucalion spoke: "Either my sagacity deceives me, or the command is one we may obey without impiety. The earth is the great parent of all; the stones are her bones; these we may cast behind us; and I think this is what the oracle means. At least, it will do no harm to try." They veiled their faces, unbound their garments, and picked up stones, and cast them behind them. The stones (wonderful to relate) began to grow soft, and assume shape. By degrees, they put on a rude resemblance to the human form, like a block half finished in the hands of the sculptor. The moisture and slime that were about them became flesh; the stony part became bones; the veins remained veins, retaining their name, only changing their use. Those thrown by the hand of the man became men, and those by the woman became women. It was a hard

race, and well adapted to labor, as we find ourselves to be at this day, giving plain indications of our origin.

Prometheus and Epimetheus were sons of Iapetus. Prometheus is a favorite subject with the poets. Aeschylus wrote three tragedies on the subjects of his confinement, his release, and his worship at Athens. Of these only the first is preserved, *Prometheus Bound*. Prometheus was the only one in the council of the gods who favored man. He alone was kind to the human race, and taught and protected them.

I formed his mind,
And through the cloud of barbarous ignorance
Diffused the beams of knowledge . . .
They saw indeed, they heard, but what availed
Or sight or hearing, all things round them rolling,
Like the unreal imagery of dreams
In wild confusion mixed!
The lightsome wall of finer masonry, the raftered roof
They knew not; but like ants still buried, delved
Deep in the earth and scooped their sunless caves.
Unmarked the seasons ranged, the biting winter,
The flower-perfumed spring, the ripening summer
Fertile of fruits.
At random all their works
Till I instructed them to mark the stars,
Their rising, and, a harder science yet, their setting.
The rich train of marshaled numbers
I taught them, and the meet array of letters.
To impress these precepts on their hearts I sent
Memory, the active mother of all reason.
I taught the patient steer to bear the yoke,
In all his toils joint-laborer of man.
By me the harnessed steed was trained to whirl
The rapid car, and grace the pride of wealth.
The tall bark, lightly bounding o'er the waves,
I taught its course, and winged its flying sail.
To man I gave these arts.

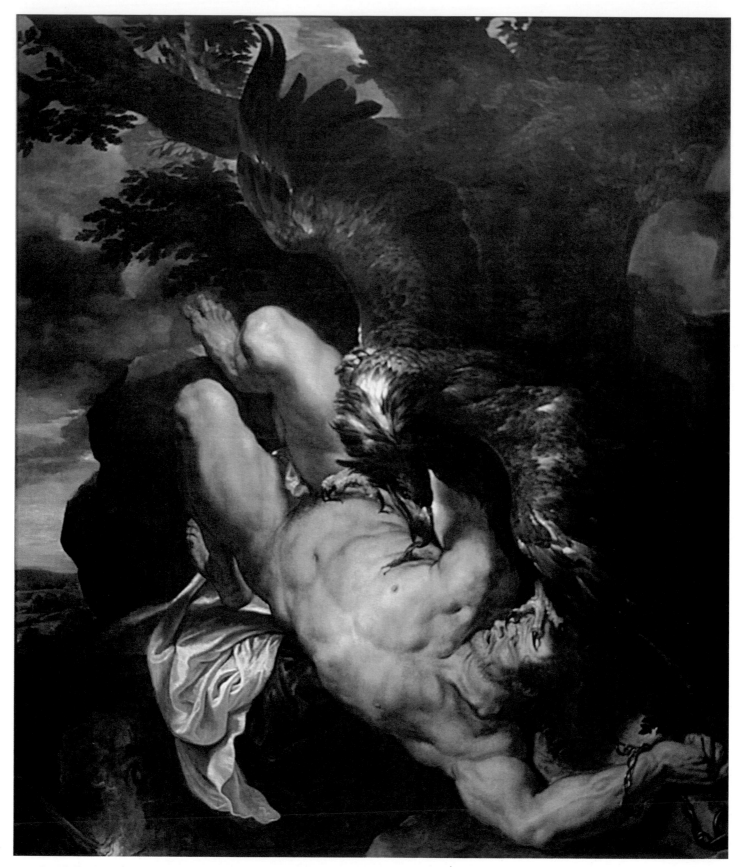

Peter Paul Rubens and Frans Snyders, *Prometheus Bound,* 1618, oil on canvas, Louvre-Lens Museum (Photograph © Jean-Pol Grandmont)

Jupiter, angry at the insolence and presumption of Prometheus in taking it upon himself to give all these blessings to man, condemned the Titan to perpetual imprisonment, bound on a rock on Mount Caucasus while a vulture should forever prey upon his liver. Prometheus might at any time have brought this state of torment to an end if he had been willing to submit to his oppressor. For Prometheus knew of a fatal marriage that Jove must make and by which he must come to ruin. Had Prometheus revealed this secret he would at once have been taken into favor. But this he disdained to do. He has therefore become the symbol of magnanimous endurance of unmerited suffering and strength of will resisting oppression.

APOLLO AND DAPHNE

Daphne was Apollo's first love. It was not brought about by accident, but by the malice of Cupid. Apollo saw the boy playing with his bow and arrows; and being himself elated with his recent victory over Python, he said to him, "What have you to do with warlike weapons, saucy boy? Leave them for hands worthy of them. Behold the conquest I have won by means of them over the vast serpent that stretched his poisonous body over acres of the plain! Be content with your torch, child, and kindle up your flames, as you call them, where you will, but presume not to meddle with my weapons." Venus's boy heard these words, and rejoined, "Your arrows may strike all things else, Apollo, but mine shall strike you." So saying, he took his stand on a rock of Parnassus and drew from his quiver two arrows of different workmanship, one to excite love, the other to repel it. The former was of gold and sharp-pointed, the latter blunt and tipped with lead. With the leaden shaft he struck the nymph Daphne, the daughter of the river god Peneus, and with the golden one Apollo, through the heart. Forthwith the god was seized with love for the maiden, and she abhorred the thought of loving. Her delight was in woodland sports and in the spoils of the chase. Many lovers sought her, but she spurned them all, ranging the woods, and taking thought neither of Cupid nor of Hymen. Her father often said to her, "Daughter, you owe me a son-in-law; you owe me grand-children." She, hating the thought of marriage as a crime, with her beautiful face tinged all over with blushes, threw her arms around her father's neck, and said, "Dearest father, grant me this favor, that I may always remain unmarried, like Diana." He consented, but at the same time said, "Your own face will forbid it." Apollo loved her, and longed to obtain her; and he who gives oracles to all in the world was not wise enough to look into his own fortunes. He saw her hair flung loose over her shoulders, and said, "If so charming in disorder, what would it be if arranged?" He saw her eyes bright as stars; he saw her lips, and was not satisfied with only seeing them. He admired her hands and arms bared to the shoulder, and whatever was hidden from view he imagined more beautiful still. He followed her; she fled, swifter than the wind, and delayed not a moment at his entreaties. "Stay," said he, "daughter of Peneus; I am not a foe. Do not fly me as a lamb flies the wolf, or a dove the hawk. It is for love I pursue you. You make me miserable, for fear you should fall and hurt yourself on these stones, and I should be the cause. Pray run slower, and I will follow slower. I am no clown, no rude peasant. Jupiter is my father, and I am lord of Delphos and Tenedos, and know all things, present and future. I am the god of song and the lyre. My arrows fly true to the mark; but alas! An arrow more fatal than mine has pierced my heart! I am the god of medicine and know the virtues of all healing plants. Alas! I suffer a malady that no balm can cure!"

The nymph continued her flight and left his plea half uttered. And even as she fled she charmed him. The wind blew her garments, and her unbound hair streamed loose behind her. The god grew impatient to find his wooings thrown away, and, sped by Cupid, gained upon her in the race. It was like a hound pursuing a hare, with open jaws ready to seize, while the feebler animal darts forward, slipping from the very grasp. So flew the god and the virgin: he on the wings of love, and she on those of fear. The pursuer is the more rapid, however, and gains upon her, and his panting breath blows upon her hair. Now her strength begins to fail, and, ready to sink, she calls upon her father,

Antonio del
Pollaiolo,
*Apollo and
Daphne,*
c. 1470,
oil on panel,
National
Gallery,
London, Wynn
Ellis Bequest

18

the river god: "Help me, Peneus! Open the earth to enclose me, or change my form, which has brought me into this danger!" Scarcely had she spoken, when a stiffness seized all her limbs; her bosom began to be enclosed in a tender bark; her hair became leaves; her arms became branches; her feet stuck fast in the ground, as roots; her face became a tree-top, retaining nothing of its former self but its beauty. Apollo stood amazed. He touched the stem and felt the flesh tremble under the new bark. He embraced the branches, and lavished kisses on the wood. The branches shrank from his lips. "Since you cannot be my wife," said he, "you shall assuredly be my tree. I will wear you for my crown. With you I will decorate my harp and my quiver; and when the great Roman conquerors lead up the triumphal pomp to the Capitol, you shall be woven into wreaths for their brows. And, as eternal youth is mine, you also shall be always green, and your leaf know no decay." The nymph, now changed into a laurel tree, bowed its head in grateful acknowledgment.

PYRAMUS AND THISBE

Pyramus was the handsomest youth, and Thisbe the fairest maiden, in all Babylonia, where Semiramis reigned. Their parents occupied adjoining houses; and the neighborhood brought the young people together, and acquaintance ripened into love. They would gladly have married, but their parents forbade it. One thing, however, they could not forbid: that love should glow with equal ardor in the bosoms of both. They conversed by signs and glances, and the fire burned more intensely for being covered up. In the wall that parted the two houses there was a crack, caused by some fault in the structure. No one had remarked it before, but the lovers discovered it. What will love not discover? It afforded a passage to the voice; and tender messages used to pass backward and forward through the gap. As they stood, Pyramus on this side, Thisbe on that, their breaths would mingle. "Cruel wall," they said, "why do you keep two lovers apart? But we will not be ungrateful. We owe you, we confess, the privilege of transmitting loving words to willing ears." Such words they uttered on

John William Waterhouse, *Thisbe,* 1909, oil on canvas, Private collection

different sides of the wall; and when night came and they must say farewell, they pressed their lips upon the wall, she on her side, he on his, as they could come no nearer. One morning, when Aurora had put out the stars, and the sun had melted the frost from the grass, they met at the accustomed spot. Then, after lamenting their hard fate, they agreed that next night, when all was still, they would slip away from watchful eyes, leave their dwellings and walk out into the fields; and to ensure a meeting, repair to a well-known edifice, standing without the city's bounds, called the tomb of Ninus, and that the one who came first should await the other at the foot of a certain tree. It was a white mulberry tree and stood near a cool spring.

All was agreed on, and they waited impatiently for the sun to go down beneath the waters and night to rise up from them. Then cautiously Thisbe stole forth, unobserved by the family, her head covered with a veil, made her way to the monument and sat down under the tree. As she sat alone in the dim light of the evening she descried a lioness, her jaws reeking with recent slaughter, approaching the fountain to slake her thirst. Thisbe fled at the sight, and sought refuge in the hollow of a rock. As she fled she dropped her veil. The lioness, after drinking at the spring, turned to retreat to the woods, and seeing the veil on the ground, tossed and rent it with her bloody mouth. Pyramus, having been delayed, now approached the place of meeting. He saw in the sand the footsteps of the lion, and the color fled from his cheeks at the sight. Presently he found the veil all rent and bloody. "Oh, hapless girl," said he, "I have been the cause of thy death! Thou, more worthy of life than I, hast fallen the first victim. I will follow. I am the guilty cause, in tempting thee forth to a place of such peril, and not being myself on the spot to guard thee. Come forth, ye lions, from the rocks, and tear this guilty body with your teeth" He took up the veil, carried it with him to the appointed tree, and covered it with kisses and with tears. "My blood also shall stain your texture," said he, and drawing his sword plunged it into his heart. The blood spurted from the wound, and tinged the white mulberries of the tree all red; and sinking into the earth reached the roots, so that the red color mounted through the trunk to the fruit. By this time, Thisbe, still trembling with fear, yet wishing not to disappoint her lover, stepped cautiously forth, looking anxiously for the youth, eager to tell him the danger she had escaped. When she came to the spot and saw the changed color of the mulberries she doubted whether it was the same place. While she hesitated she saw the form of one struggling in the agonies of death. She started back; a shudder ran through her frame as a ripple on the face of the still water when a sudden breeze sweeps over it. But as soon as she recognized her lover, she screamed and beat her breast; embracing the lifeless body, pouring tears into its wounds, and imprinting kisses on the cold lips. "Oh, Pyramus," she cried, "what has done this? Answer me, Pyramus; it is your own Thisbe that speaks. Hear me, dearest, and lift that drooping head!" At the name of Thisbe, Pyramus opened his eyes, then closed them again. She saw her veil stained with blood and the scabbard empty of its sword. "Thy own hand has slain thee, and for my sake," she said. "I too can be brave for once, and my love is as strong as thine. I will follow thee in death, for I have been the cause; and death, which alone could part us, shall not prevent my joining thee. And ye, unhappy parents of us both, deny us not our united request. As love and death have joined us, let one tomb contain us. And thou, tree, retain the marks of slaughter. Let thy berries still serve for memorials of our blood." So saying, she plunged the sword into her breast. Her parents acceded to her wish; the gods also ratified it. The two bodies were buried in one sepulcher, and the tree ever after brought forth purple berries, as it does to this day.

CEPHALUS AND PROCRIS

Cephalus was a beautiful youth and fond of manly sports. He would rise before the dawn to pursue the chase. Aurora saw him when she first looked forth, fell in love with him, and stole him away. But Cephalus was just married to a charming wife whom he loved devotedly. Her name was Procris. She was a favorite of Diana, the goddess of hunting, who had given her a dog, which could outrun every rival, and a javelin, which would never fail of its mark; and Procris gave these presents to her husband. Cephalus was so happy in his wife that he resisted all the entreaties of Aurora, and she finally dismissed him in displeasure, saying, "Go, ungrateful mortal, keep your wife, whom, if I am not much mistaken, you will one day be very sorry you ever saw again." Cephalus returned, and was as happy as ever in his wife and his woodland sports. Now it happened some angry deity had sent a ravenous fox to annoy the country; and the hunters turned out in great strength to capture it. Their efforts were all in vain; no dog could run it down; and at last they came to Cephalus to borrow his famous dog, whose name was Lelaps. No sooner was the dog let loose than he darted off, quicker than their eye could follow him. If they had not seen his footprints in the sand they would have thought he flew. Cephalus and others stood on a hill and saw the race. The fox tried every art; he ran in a circle and turned on his track, the dog close upon him, with open jaws, snapping at his heels, but biting only the air. Cephalus was about to use his javelin, when suddenly he saw both dog and game stop instantly. The heavenly powers who had given both, were not willing that either should conquer. In the very attitude of life and action they were turned into stone. So lifelike and natural did they look, you would have thought, as you looked at them, that one was going to bark, the other to leap forward.

Cephalus, though he had lost his dog, still continued to take delight in the chase. He would go out at early morning, ranging the woods and hills unaccompanied by any one, needing no help, for his javelin was a sure weapon in all cases. Fatigued with hunting, when the sun got high he would seek a shady nook where a cool stream flowed, and, stretched on the grass with his garments thrown aside, would enjoy the breeze. Sometimes he would say aloud, "Come, sweet breeze, come and fan my breast, come and allay the heat that burns me." Some one passing by one day heard him talking in this way to the air, and, foolishly believing that he was talking to some maiden, went and told the secret to Procris, Cephalus's wife. Love is credulous. Procris, at the sudden shock, fainted away. Presently recovering, she said, "It cannot be true; I will not believe it unless I myself am a witness to it." So she waited, with anxious heart, until the next morning, when Cephalus went to hunt as usual. Then she stole out after him, and concealed herself in the place where the informer directed her. Cephalus came as he was wont when tired with sport, and stretched himself on the green bank, saying, "Come, sweet breeze, come and fan me; you know how I love you!

You make the groves and my solitary rambles delightful." He was running on in this way when he heard, or thought he heard, a sound as of a sob in the bushes. Supposing it some wild animal, he threw his javelin at the spot. A cry from his beloved Procris told him that the weapon had too surely met its mark. He rushed to the place, and found her bleeding and with sinking strength endeavoring to draw forth from the wound the javelin, her own gift. Cephalus raised her from the earth, strove to stanch the blood, and called her to revive and not to leave him miserable, to reproach himself with her death. She opened her feeble eyes, and forced herself to utter these few words: "I implore you,

Cephalus and Procris, c. 1650, oil on canvas, National Museum of Slovenia

if you have ever loved me, if I have ever deserved kindness at your hands, my husband, grant me this last request; do not marry that odious Breeze!" This disclosed the whole mystery; but alas! What advantage to disclose it now? She died; but her face wore a calm expression, and she looked pityingly and forgivingly on her husband when he made her understand the truth.

CHAPTER III: IO AND CALLISTO. DIANA AND ACTAEON. THE STORY OF PHAETON.

IO

Jupiter and Juno, although husband and wife, did not live together very happily. Jupiter did not love his wife very much, and Juno distrusted her husband and was always accusing him of unfaithfulness. One day she perceived that it suddenly grew dark, and immediately suspected that her husband had raised a cloud to hide some of his doings that would not bear the light. She brushed away the cloud and saw her husband on the banks of a glassy river, with a beautiful heifer standing near him. Juno suspected that the heifer's form concealed some fair nymph of mortal mold. This was indeed the case; for it was Io, the daughter of the river god Inachus, whom Jupiter had been flirting with, and, when he became aware of the approach of his wife, had changed into that form. Juno joined her husband, and noticing the heifer, praised its beauty, and asked whose it was, and of what herd. Jupiter, to stop her questions, replied that it was a fresh creation from the earth. Juno asked to have it as a gift. What could Jupiter do? He was loath to give his mistress to his wife; yet how to refuse so trifling a present as a simple heifer? He could not, without arousing suspicion; so he consented. The goddess was not yet relieved of her suspicions, and she delivered the heifer to Argus, to be strictly watched. Now Argus had a hundred eyes in his head and never went to sleep with more than two at a time, so that he kept watch of Io constantly. He suf-

fered her to feed through the day, and at night tied her up with a vile rope round her neck. She would have stretched out her arms to implore freedom of Argus, but she had no arms to stretch out, and her voice was a bellow that frightened even herself. She saw her father and her sisters, went near them, and suffered them to pat her back, and heard them admire her beauty. Her father reached her a tuft of grass, and she licked the outstretched hand. She longed to make herself known to him and would have uttered her wish; but, alas! words were

Abraham Bloemaert, *Mercury, Argus and Io*, c. 1592, Central Museum of Utrecht

wanting. At length she bethought herself of writing and inscribed her name, it was a short one, with her hoof on the sand. Inachus recognized it, and discovering that his daughter, whom he had long sought in vain, was hidden under this disguise, mourned over her, and, embracing her white neck, exclaimed, "Alas! My daughter, it would have been a less grief to have lost you altogether!" While he thus lamented, Argus, observing, came and drove her away and took his seat on a high bank, whence he could see in every direction.

Jupiter was troubled at beholding the sufferings of his mistress, and calling Mercury, told him to go and dispatch Argus. Mercury made haste, put his winged slippers on his feet, and cap on his head, took his sleep-producing wand, and leaped down from the heavenly towers to the earth. There he laid aside his wings, and kept only his wand, with which he presented himself as a shepherd driving his flock. As he strolled on he blew upon his pipes. These were what are called the Syrinx or Pan pipes.

Argus listened with delight, for he had never heard the instrument before. "Young man," said he, "come and take a seat by me on this stone. There is no better place for your flock to graze in than hereabouts, and here is a pleasant shade such as shepherds love." Mercury sat down, talked, and told stories until it grew late, and played upon his pipes his most soothing strains, hoping to lull the watchful eyes to sleep, but all in vain; for Argus still contrived to keep some of his eyes open, though he shut the rest. Among other stories, Mercury told him how the instrument on which he played was invented. "There was a certain nymph, whose name was Syrinx, who was much beloved by the satyrs and spirits of the wood; but she would have none of them. She was a faithful worshipper of Diana and followed the chase. You would have thought it was Diana herself, had you seen her in her hunting dress, only that her bow was of horn and Diana's of silver. One day, as she was returning from the chase, Pan met her, told her just this and added more of the same sort. She ran away, without stopping to hear his compliments, and he pursued until she came to the bank of

the river, where he overtook her, and she had only time to call for help on her friends, the water nymphs. They heard and consented. Pan threw his arms around what he supposed to be the form of the nymph, and found he embraced only a tuft of reeds! As he breathed a sigh, the air sounded through the reeds, and produced a plaintive melody. The god, charmed with the novelty and with the sweetness of the music, said 'Thus, then, at least, you shall be mine.' And he took some of the reeds, and placing them together, of unequal lengths, side by side, made an instrument which he called Syrinx, in honor of the nymph." Before Mercury had finished his story, he saw Argus's eyes all asleep. As his head nodded forward on his breast, Mercury with one stroke cut his neck through and tumbled his head down the rocks. O hapless Argus! The light of your hundred eyes is quenched at once! Juno took them and put them as ornaments on the tail of her peacock, where they remain to this day.

But the vengeance of Juno was not yet satiated. She sent a gadfly to torment Io, who fled over the whole world from its pursuit. She swam through the Ionian Sea, which derived its name from her, then roamed over the plains of Illyria, ascended Mount Haemus, and crossed the Thracian strait, thence named the Bosphorus (cow-bearer), rambled on through Scythia and the country of the Cimmerians, and arrived at last on the banks of the Nile. At length Jupiter interceded for her, and, upon his promising not to pay her any more attentions, Juno consented to restore her to her form. It was curious to see her gradually recover her former self. The coarse hairs fell from her body, her horns shrunk up, her eyes grew narrower, her mouth shorter; hands and fingers came instead of hoofs to her forefeet; in fine, there was nothing left of the heifer except her beauty. At first she was afraid to speak for fear she should low, but gradually she recovered her confidence, and was restored to her father and sisters.

CALLISTO

Callisto was another maiden who excited the jealousy of Juno, and the goddess changed her into a bear. "I will take away," said she, "that beauty with which you have captivated my husband." Down fell Callisto on her hands and knees; she tried to stretch out her arms in supplication, they were already beginning to be covered with black hair. Her hands grew rounded, became armed with crooked claws, and served for feet; her mouth, which Jove used to praise for its beauty, became a horrid pair of jaws; her voice, which if unchanged would have moved the heart to pity, became a growl, more fit to inspire terror. Yet her former disposition remained, and, with continued groaning, she bemoaned her fate, and stood upright as well as she could, lifting up her paws to beg for mercy; and felt that Jove was unkind, though she could not tell him so. Ah, how often, afraid to stay in the woods all night alone, she wandered about the neighborhood of her former haunts; how often, frightened by the dogs, did she, so lately a huntress, fly in terror from the hunters! Often she fled from the wild beasts, forgetting that she was now a wild beast herself; and, bear as she was, was afraid of the bears. One day a youth espied her as he was hunting. She saw him and recognized him as her own son, now grown a young man. She stopped, and felt inclined to embrace him. As she was about to approach, he, alarmed, raised his hunting spear, and was on the point of transfixing her, when Jupiter, beholding, arrested the crime, and, snatching away both of them, placed them in the heavens as the Great and Little Bear. Juno was in a rage to see her rival so set in honor and hastened to ancient Tethys and Oceanus, the powers of ocean, and, in answer to their inquiries, thus told the cause of her coming: "Do you ask why I, the queen of the gods, have left the heavenly plains and sought your depths. Learn that I am supplanted in heaven; my place is given to another. You will hardly believe me; but look when night darkens the world, and you shall see the two, of whom I have so much reason to complain, exalted to the heavens, in that part where the circle is the smallest, in the neighborhood of the pole. Why should any one hereafter tremble at the thought of offending Juno, when such rewards are the consequence of my displeasure! See what I have been able to effect! I forbade her to wear the human form; she is placed among the stars! So do my punishments result, such is the extent of my power! Better that she should have resumed her former shape, as I permitted Io to do. Perhaps he means

to marry her, and put me away! But you, my foster parents, if you feel for me, and see with displeasure this unworthy treatment of me, show it, I beseech you, by forbidding this guilty couple from coming into your waters." The powers of the ocean assented, and consequently the two constellations of the Great and Little Bear move round and round in heaven, but never sink, as the other stars do, beneath the ocean. The last star in the tail of the Little Bear is the Pole star, the guide of mariners, called also the Cynosure.

DIANA AND ACTAEON

It was midday, and the sun stood equally distant from either goal, when young Actaeon, son of King Cadmus, thus addressed the youths who with him were hunting the stag in the mountains: "Friends, our nets and our weapons are wet with the blood of our victims; we have had sport enough for one day, and tomorrow we can renew our labors. Now, while Phoebus parches the earth, let us put by our instruments and indulge ourselves with rest." There was a valley thickly enclosed with cypresses and pines, sacred to the huntress-queen, Diana. In the extremity of the valley was a cave, not adorned with art, but nature had counterfeited art in its construction, for she had turned the arch of its roof with stones as delicately fitted as if by the hand of man. A fountain burst out from one side, whose open basin was bounded by a grassy rim. Here the goddess of the woods used to come when weary with hunting and lave her virgin limbs in the sparkling water. One day, having repaired thither with her nymphs, she handed her javelin, her quiver, and her bow to one, her robe to another, while a third unbound the sandals from her feet. Then Crocale, the most skillful of them, arranged her hair, and Nephele, Hyale, and the rest drew water in capacious urns. While the goddess was thus employed in the labors of the toilet, behold, Actaeon, having quitted his companions, and rambling without any especial object, came to the place, led thither by his destiny.

As he presented himself at the entrance of the cave, the nymphs, seeing a man, screamed and rushed towards the goddess to hide her with their bodies. But she was taller than the rest, and overtopped them all by a head. Such a color as tinges the clouds at sunset or at dawn came over the countenance of Diana thus taken by surprise. Surrounded as she was by her nymphs, she yet turned half away and sought with a sudden impulse for her arrows. As they were not at hand, she dashed the water into the face of the intruder, adding these words: "Now go and tell, if you can, that you have seen Diana unclothed." Immediately a pair of branching stag's horns grew out of his head, his neck gained in length, his ears grew sharp-pointed, his hands became feet, his arms long legs, his body was covered with a hairy spotted hide. Fear took the place of his former boldness, and the hero fled. He could not but admire his own speed; but when he saw his horns in the water, "Ah, wretched me!" he would have said, but no sound followed the effort. He groaned, and tears flowed down the face that had taken the place of his own. Yet his consciousness remained. What shall he do? Go home to seek the palace, or lie hid in the woods? The latter he was afraid, the former he was ashamed, to do. While he hesitated the dogs saw him. First Melampus, a Spartan dog, gave the signal with his bark, then Pamphagus, Dorceus, Lelaps, Theron, Nape, Tigris, and all the rest, rushed after him swifter than the wind. Over rocks and cliffs, through mountain gorges that seemed impracticable, he fled, and they followed. Where he had often chased the stag and cheered on his pack, his pack now chased him, cheered on by his own huntsmen. He longed to cry out, "I am Actaeon; recognize your master!" But the words came not at his will. The air resounded with the bark of the dogs. Presently one fastened on his back, another seized his shoulder. While they held their master, the rest of the pack came up and buried their teeth in his flesh. He groaned, not in a human voice, yet certainly not in a stag's, and, falling on

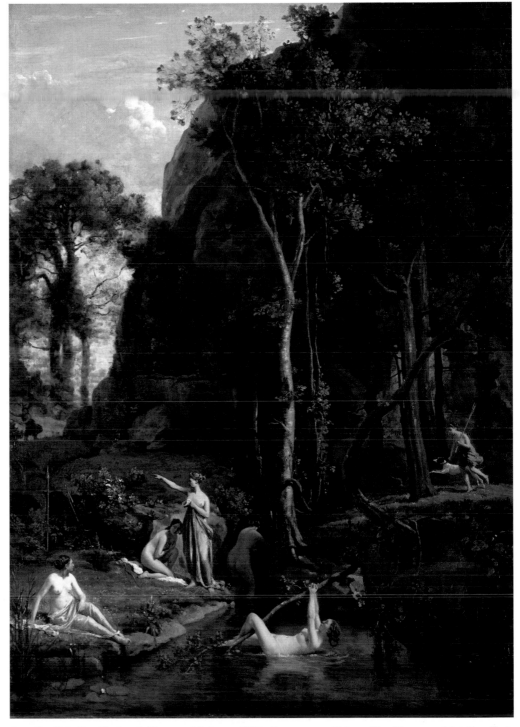

Jean-Baptiste-Camille Corot, *Diana and Actaeon*, 1836, oil on canvas, Metropolitan Museum of Art, New York

his knees, raised his eyes, and would have raised his arms in supplication, if he had had them. His friends and fellow-huntsmen cheered on the dogs, and looked everywhere for Actaeon, calling on him to join the sport. At the sound of his name, he turned his head, and heard them regret that he should be away. He earnestly wished he were. He would have been well pleased to see the exploits of his dogs, but to feel them was too much. They were all around him, rending and tearing; and it was not until they had torn his life out that the anger of Diana was satisfied.

LATONA AND THE RUSTICS

Some thought the goddess in this instance more severe than was just, while others praised her conduct as strictly consistent with her virgin dignity. As usual, the recent event brought older ones to mind, and one of the bystanders told this story. "Some countrymen of Lycia once insulted the goddess Latona, but not with impunity. When I was young, my father, who had grown too old for active labors, sent me to Lycia to drive thence some choice oxen, and there I saw the very pond and marsh where the wonder happened. Near-by stood an ancient altar, black with the smoke of sacrifice and almost buried among the reeds. I inquired whose altar it might be, whether of Faunus or the Naiads or some god of the neighboring mountain, and one of the country people replied, 'No mountain or river god possesses this altar, but she whom royal Juno in her jealousy drove from land to land, denying her any spot of earth whereon to rear her twins. Bearing in her arms the infant deities, Latona reached this land, weary with her burden and parched with thirst. By chance she espied in the bottom of the valley this pond of clear water, where the country people were at work gathering willows and osiers. The goddess approached, and kneeling on the bank would have slaked her thirst in the cool stream, but the rustics forbade her. 'Why do you refuse me water?' said she; 'water is free to all. Nature allows no one to claim as property the sunshine, the air, or the water. I come to take my share of the common blessing. Yet I ask it of you as a favor. I have no intention of washing my limbs in it, weary though they be, but only to quench my thirst. My mouth is so dry that I can hardly speak. A draught of water would be nectar to me; it would revive me, and I would own myself indebted to you for life itself. Let these infants move your pity, who stretch out their little arms as if to plead for me;' and the children, as it happened, were stretching out their arms. Who would not have been moved with these gentle words of the goddess? But these clowns persisted in their rudeness; they even added jeers and threats of violence if she did not leave the place. Nor was this all. They waded into the pond and stirred up the mud with their feet, so as to make the water unfit to drink. Latona was so angry that she ceased to feel her thirst. She no longer supplicated the clowns, but lifting her hands to heaven exclaimed, 'May they never quit that pool, but pass their lives there!' And it came to pass accordingly. They now live in the water, sometimes totally submerged, then raising their heads above the surface, or swimming upon it. Sometimes they come out upon the bank, but soon leap back again into the water. They still use their base voices in railing, and though they have the water all to themselves, are not ashamed to croak in the midst of it. Their voices are harsh, their throats bloated, their mouths have become stretched by constant railing, their necks have shrunk up and disappeared, and their heads are joined to their bodies. Their backs are green, their disproportioned bellies white, and in short they are now frogs, and dwell in the slimy pool." The persecution that Latona experienced from Juno is alluded to in the story. The tradition was that the future mother of Apollo and Diana, flying from the wrath of Juno, besought all the islands of the Aegean to afford her a place of rest, but all feared too much the potent queen of heaven to assist her rival. Delos alone consented to become the birthplace of the future deities. Delos was then a floating island; but when Latona arrived there, Jupiter fastened it with adamantine chains to the bottom of the sea, that it might be a secure resting place for his beloved.

PHAETON

Epaphus was the son of Jupiter and Io. Phaeton, child of the Sun, was one day boasting to him of his high descent and of his father Phoebus. Epaphus could not bear it. "Foolish fellow," said he "you believe your mother in all things, and you are puffed up by your pride in a false father." Phaeton went in rage and shame and reported this to his mother, Clymene. "If," said he, "I am indeed of heavenly birth, give me, mother, some proof of it, and establish my claim to the honor." Clymene stretched forth her hands towards the skies, and said, "I call to witness the Sun which looks down upon us, that I have told you the truth. If I speak falsely, let this be the last time I behold his light. But it needs not much labor to go and inquire for yourself; the land whence the sun rises lies next to ours. Go and demand of him whether he will own you as a son," Phaeton heard with delight. He traveled to India, which lies directly in the regions of sunrise; and, full of hope and pride, approached the goal whence the Sun begins his course. The palace of the Sun stood reared aloft on columns, glittering with gold and precious stones, while polished ivory formed the ceilings, and silver the doors. The workmanship surpassed the material; for upon the walls Vulcan had represented earth, sea and skies, with their inhabitants. In the sea were the nymphs, some sporting in the waves, some riding on the backs of fishes, while others sat upon the rocks and dried their sea-green hair. Their faces were not all alike, nor yet unlike, but such as sisters' ought to be. The earth had its towns and forests and rivers and rustic divinities. Over all was carved the likeness of the glorious heaven, and on the silver doors the twelve signs of the zodiac, six on each side.

Clymene's son advanced up the steep ascent, and entered the halls of his disputed father. He approached the paternal presence but stopped at a distance, for the light was more than he could bear. Phoebus, arrayed in purple vesture, sat on a throne that glittered as with diamonds. On his right hand and his left stood the Day, the Month, and the Year, and, at regular intervals, the Hours. Spring stood with her head crowned with flowers, and Summer, with garment cast aside, and a garland formed of spears of ripened grain, and Autumn, with his feet stained with grape juice, and icy Winter, with his hair stiffened with hoar frost. Surrounded by these attendants, the Sun, with

the eye that sees every thing, beheld the youth dazzled with the novelty and splendor of the scene, and inquired the purpose of his errand. The youth replied, "Oh, light of the boundless world, Phoebus, my father, if you permit me to use that name, give me some proof, I beseech you, by which I may be known as yours." He ceased; and his father, laying aside the beams that shone all around his head, bade him approach, and embracing him, said, "My son, you deserve not to be disowned, and I confirm what your mother has told you. To put an end to your doubts, ask what you will, the gift shall be yours. I call to witness that dreadful lake, which I never saw, but which we gods swear by in our most solemn engagements." Phaeton immediately asked to be permitted for one day to drive the chariot of the sun. The father repented of his promise; thrice and four times he shook his radiant head in warning. "I have spoken rashly," said he; "only this request I would fain deny. I beg you to withdraw it. It is not a safe boon, nor one, my Phaeton, suited to your youth and strength. Your lot is mortal, and you ask what is beyond a mortal's power. In your ignorance you aspire to do that which not even the gods themselves may do. None but myself may drive the flaming car of day; not even Jupiter, whose terrible right arm hurls the thunderbolts. The first part of the way is steep, and such as the horses when fresh in the morning can hardly climb; the middle is high up in the heavens, whence I myself can scarcely, without alarm, look down and behold the earth and sea stretched beneath me. The last part of the road descends rapidly, and requires most careful driving. Tethys, who is waiting to receive me, often trembles for me lest I should fall headlong. Add to all this, the heaven is all the time turning round and carrying the stars with it. I have to be perpetually on my guard lest that movement, which sweeps everything else along, should hurry me also away. Suppose I should lend you the chariot, what would you do? Could you keep your course while the sphere was revolving under you? Perhaps you think that there are forests and cities, the abodes of gods, and palaces and temples on the way. On the contrary, the road is through the midst of frightful monsters. You pass by the horns of the Bull, in front of the Archer, and near the Lion's jaws, and where the Scorpion stretches its arms in one direction and the Crab in another. Nor will you find it easy to guide those horses, with their breasts full of fire that they breathe forth from their mouths and nostrils. I can scarcely govern them myself, when they are unruly and resist the reins. Beware, my son, lest I should give you a fatal gift; recall your request while yet you may. Do you ask me for proof that you are sprung from my blood? I give you a proof in my fears for you. Look at my face, I would that you could look into my breast; you would there see all a father's anxiety. Finally," he continued, "look round the world and choose whatever you will of what earth or sea contains most precious, ask it and fear no refusal. This only I pray you not to urge. It is not honor, but destruction you seek. Why do you hang round my neck and still entreat me? You shall have it if you persist, the oath is sworn and must be kept, but I beg you to choose more wisely." He ended; but the youth rejected all admonition and held to his demand.

So, having resisted as long as he could, Phoebus at last led the way to where stood the lofty chariot. It was of gold, the gift of Vulcan; the axle was of gold, the pole and wheels of gold, the spokes of silver. Along the seat were rows of chrysolites and diamonds, which reflected all around the brightness of the sun. While the daring youth gazed in admiration, the early Dawn threw open the purple doors of the east, and showed the pathway strewn with roses. The stars withdrew, marshaled by the Daystar, which last of all retired also. The father, when he saw the earth beginning to glow, and the Moon preparing to retire, ordered the Hours to harness up the horses. They obeyed, and led forth from the lofty stalls the steeds full fed with ambrosia, and attached the reins. Then the father bathed the face of his son with a powerful unguent, making him capable of enduring the brightness of the flame. He set the rays on his head, and, with a foreboding sigh, said, "If, my son, you will in this at least heed my advice, spare the whip and hold tight the reins. They go fast enough of their own

accord; the labor is to hold them in. You are not to take the straight road directly between the five circles, but turn off to the left. Keep within the limit of the middle zone, and avoid the northern and the southern alike. You will see the marks of the wheels, and they will serve to guide you. And, that the skies and the earth may each receive their due share of heat, go not too high, or you will burn the heavenly dwellings, nor too low, or you will set the earth on fire; the middle course is safest and best. And now I leave you to your chance, which I hope will plan better for you than you have done for yourself. Night is passing out of the western gates and we can delay no longer. Take the reins; but if at last your heart fails you, and you will benefit by my advice, stay where you are in safety, and suffer me to light and warm the earth." The agile youth sprang into the chariot, stood erect and grasped the reins with delight, pouring out thanks to his reluctant parent.

Meanwhile the horses fill the air with their snortings and fiery breath, and stamp the ground impatient. Now the bars are let down, and the boundless plain of the universe lies open before them. They dart forward and cleave the opposing clouds, and outrun the morning breezes that started from the same eastern goal. The steeds soon perceived that the load they drew was lighter than usual; and as a ship without ballast is tossed hither and thither on the sea, so the chariot, without its accustomed weight, was dashed about as if empty. They rush headlong and leave the traveled road. He is alarmed, and knows not how to guide them; nor, if he knew, has he the power. Then, for the first time, the Great and Little Bear were scorched with heat, and would fain, if it were possible, have plunged into the water; and the Serpent which lies coiled up round the north pole, torpid and harmless, grew warm, and with warmth felt its rage revive. Boötes, they say, fled away, though encumbered with his plow, and all unused to rapid motion. When hapless Phaeton looked down upon the earth, now spreading in vast extent beneath him, he grew pale and his knees shook with terror. In spite of the glare all around him, the sight of his eyes grew dim. He wished

Nicolas Bertin, *Phaeton on the Chariot of Apollo,* Late seventeenth – early eighteenth century

he had never touched his father's horses, never learned his parentage, never prevailed in his request. He is borne along like a vessel that flies before a tempest, when the pilot can do no more and betakes himself to his prayers. What shall he do? Much of the heavenly road is left behind, but more remains before. He turns his eyes from one direction to the other; now to the goal whence he began his course, now to the realms of sunset that he is not destined to reach. He loses his self-command and knows not what to do, whether to draw tight the reins or throw them loose; he forgets the names of the horses. He sees with terror the monstrous forms scattered over the surface of heaven. Here

the Scorpion extended his two great arms, with his tail and crooked claws stretching over two signs of the zodiac. When the boy beheld him, reeking with poison and menacing with his fangs, his courage failed, and the reins fell from his hands. The horses, feeling the reins loose on their backs, dashed headlong, and unrestrained went off into unknown regions of the sky, in among the stars, hurling the chariot over pathless places, now up in high heaven, now down almost to the earth. The moon saw with astonishment her brother's chariot running beneath her own. The clouds begin to smoke, and the mountaintops take fire; the fields are parched with heat, the plants wither, the trees with their leafy branches burn, the harvest is ablaze! But these are small things. Great cities perished, with their walls and towers; whole nations with their people were consumed to ashes! The forest-clad mountains burned, Athos and Taurus and Tmolus; Ida, once celebrated for fountains, but now all dry; the Muses' mountain Helicon, and Haemus; Aetna, with fires within and without, and Parnassus, with his two peaks, and Rhodope, forced at last to part with his snowy crown. Her cold climate was no protection to Scythia, Caucasus burned, and Ossa and Pindus, and, greater than both, Olympus; the Alps high in air, and the Apennines crowned with clouds. Then Phaeton beheld the world on fire, and felt the heat intolerable. The air he breathed was like the air of a furnace and full of burning ashes, and the smoke was of a pitchy darkness. He dashed forward he knew not whither. Then, it is believed, the people of Aethiopia became black by the blood being forced so suddenly to the surface, and the Libyan desert was dried up to the condition in which it remains to this day. The Nymphs of the fountains, with disheveled hair, mourned their waters, nor were the rivers safe beneath their banks; Tanais smoked, and Caicus, Xanthus and Meander. Babylonian Euphrates and Ganges, Tagus with golden sands, and Caijster where the swans resort. Nile fled away and hid his head in the desert, and there it still remains concealed. Where he used to discharge his waters through seven mouths into the sea, there seven dry channels alone remained. The earth cracked open, and through the chinks light broke into Tartarus and frightened the king of shadows and his queen. The sea shrank up. Where before was water, it became a dry plain; and the mountains that lie beneath the waves lifted up their heads and became islands. The fishes sought the lowest depths, and the dolphins no longer ventured as usual to sport on the surface. Even Nereus, and his wife Doris, with the Nereids, their daughters, sought the deepest caves for refuge. Thrice Neptune essayed to raise his head above the surface and thrice was driven back by the heat. Earth, surrounded as she was by waters, yet with head and shoulders bare, screening her face with her hand, looked up to heaven, and with a husky voice called on Jupiter. "O ruler of the gods, if I have deserved this treatment, and it is your will that I perish with fire, why withhold your thunderbolts? Let me at least fall by your hand. Is this the reward of my fertility, of my obedient service? Is it for this that I have supplied herbage for cattle, and fruits for men, and frankincense for your altars? But if I am unworthy of regard, what has my brother Ocean done to deserve such a fate? If neither of us can excite your pity, think, I pray you, of your own heaven, and behold how both the poles are smoking which sustain your palace, which must fall if they be destroyed. Atlas faints, and scarce holds up his burden. If sea, earth, and heaven perish, we fall into ancient Chaos. Save what yet remains to us from the devouring flame. Oh, take thought for our deliverance in this awful moment!" Thus spoke Earth, and overcome with heat and thirst, could say no more. Then Jupiter Omnipotent, calling to witness all the gods, including him who had lent the chariot, and showing them that all was lost unless some speedy remedy were applied, mounted the lofty tower from whence he diffuses clouds over the earth, and hurls the forked lightnings. But at that time not a cloud was to be found to interpose for a screen to earth, nor was a shower remaining unexhausted. He thundered, and brandishing a lightning-bolt in his right hand launched it against the charioteer, and struck him at the same moment from his seat and from existence!

Phaeton, with his hair on fire, fell headlong, like a shooting star which marks the heavens with its brightness as it falls, and Eridanus, the great river, received him and cooled his burning frame. The Italian Naiads reared a tomb for him, and inscribed these words upon the stone: "Driver of Phoebus' chariot, Phaeton, Struck by Jove's thunder, rests beneath this stone. He could not rule his father's car of fire, Yet was it much so nobly to aspire." His sisters, the Heliades, as they lamented his fate were turned into poplar trees, on the banks of the river, and their tears, which continued to flow, became amber as they dropped into the stream.

CHAPTER IV: MIDAS. BAUCIS AND PHILEMON. PLUTO AND PROSERPINE.

MIDAS

Bacchus, on a certain occasion, found his old school master and foster father, Silenus, missing. The old man had been drinking, and in that state had wandered away, and was found by some peasants, who carried him to their king, Midas. Midas recognized him, and treated him hospitably, entertaining him for ten days and nights with an unceasing round of jollity. On the eleventh day he brought Silenus back and restored him in safety to his pupil. Whereupon Bacchus offered Midas his choice of whatever reward he might wish. He asked that whatever he might touch should be changed into gold. Bacchus consented, though sorry that he had not made a better choice. Midas went his way, rejoicing in his newly acquired power, which he hastened to put to the test. He could scarce believe his eyes when he found that a twig of an oak, which he plucked from the branch, became gold in his hand. He took up a stone; it changed to gold. He touched a sod; it did the same. He took an apple from the tree; you would have thought he had robbed the garden of the Hesperides. His joy knew no bounds, and as soon as he got home, he ordered the servants to set a splendid repast on the table. Then he found to his dismay that whether he touched bread, it hardened in his hand; or put a morsel to his lips, it defied his teeth. He took a glass of wine, but it flowed down his throat like melted gold. In consternation at the unprecedented affliction, he strove to divest himself of his power; he hated the gift he had lately coveted. But all in vain; starvation seemed to await him. He raised his arms, all shining with gold, in prayer to Bacchus, begging to be delivered from his glittering destruction. Bacchus, merciful deity, heard and consented. "Go," said he, "to the river Pactolus, trace the stream to its fountainhead, there plunge in your head and body and wash away your fault and its punishment." He did so, and scarce had he touched the waters before the gold-creating power passed into them, and the river sands became changed into gold, as they remain to this day.

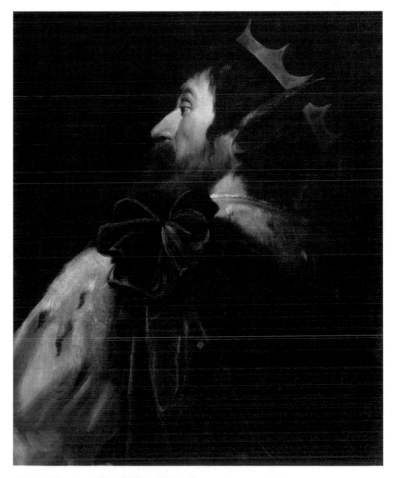

Andrea Vaccaro, *King Midas*, 1670, oil on canvas

31

Thenceforth Midas, hating wealth and splendor, dwelt in the country, and became a worshipper of Pan, the god of the fields. On a certain occasion Pan had the temerity to compare his music with that of Apollo and to challenge the god of the lyre to a trial of skill. The challenge was accepted, and Tmolus, the mountain-god, was chosen umpire. Tmolus took his seat and cleared away the trees from his ears to listen. At a given signal Pan blew on his pipes, and with his rustic melody gave great satisfaction to himself and his faithful follower, Midas, who happened to be present. Then Tmolus turned his head toward the sun god, and all his trees turned with him. Apollo rose, his brow wreathed with Parnassian laurel, while his robe of Tyrian purple swept the ground. In his left hand he held the lyre, and with his right hand struck the strings. Ravished with the harmony, Tmolus at once awarded the victory to the god of the lyre, and all but Midas acquiesced in the judgment. He dissented and questioned the justice of the award. Apollo would not suffer such a depraved pair of ears any longer to wear the human form but caused them to increase in length, grow hairy, within and without, and to become movable, on their roots; in short, to be on the perfect pattern of those of an ass. Mortified enough was King Midas at this mishap; but he consoled himself with the thought that it was possible to hide his misfortune, which he attempted to do by means of an ample turban or headdress. But his hairdresser of course knew the secret. He was charged not to mention it and threatened with dire punishment if he presumed to disobey. But he found it too much for his discretion to keep such a secret; so he went out into the meadow, dug a hole in the ground, and stooping down, whispered the story, and covered it up. Before long a thick bed of reeds sprang up in the meadow, and as soon as it had gained its growth, began whispering the story, and has continued to do so, from that day to this, with every breeze that passes over the place. The story of King Midas has been told by others with some variations.

Midas was king of Phrygia. He was the son of Gordius, a poor countryman, who was taken by the people and made king, in obedience to the command of the oracle, which had said that their future king should come in a wagon. While the people were deliberating, Gordius with his wife and son came driving his wagon into the public square. Gordius, being made king, dedicated his wagon to the deity of the oracle and tied it up in its place with a fast knot. This was the celebrated Gordian knot, of which, in after times it was said, that whoever should untie it should become lord of all Asia. Many tried, but none succeeded, until Alexander the Great, in his career of conquest, came to Phrygia. He tried his skill with as ill success as the others, until growing impatient he drew his sword and cut the knot. When he afterwards succeeded in subjecting all Asia to his sway, people began to think that he had complied with the terms of the oracle according to its true meaning.

BAUCIS AND PHILEMON

On a certain hill in Phrygia stand a linden tree and an oak, enclosed by a low wall. Not far from the spot is a marsh, formerly good habitable land, but now indented with pools, the resort of fen-birds and cormorants. Once upon a time, Jupiter, in human shape, visited this country, and with him his son Mercury (he of the caduceus) without his wings. They presented themselves at many a door as weary travelers, seeking rest and shelter, but found all closed, for it was late, and the inhospitable inhabitants would not rouse themselves to open for their reception. At last a humble dwelling received them, a small thatched cottage, where Baucis, a pious old dame, and her husband Philemon, united when young, had grown old together. Not ashamed of their poverty, they made it endurable by moderate desires and kind dispositions. One need not look there for master or for servant; they two were the whole household, master and servant alike. When the two heavenly guests crossed the humble threshold and bowed their heads to pass under the low door, the old man placed a seat, on which Baucis, bustling and attentive, spread a cloth, and begged them to sit down. Then she raked out the coals from the ashes, kindled up a fire, and fed it with leaves and dry bark, and with her scanty breath blew it into a flame. She brought out of a corner split sticks and dry branches, broke them up, and

Philemon and Baucis, Circle of Andrea Appiani, oil on canvas

Hades Abducting Persephone, Fresco from the royal tomb at Verginia, Macedonia, Greece, 340 BCE

placed them under the small kettle. Her husband collected some potherbs in the garden, and she shred them from the stalks and prepared them for the pot. He reached down with a forked stick a flitch of bacon hanging in the chimney, cut a small piece, and put it in the pot to boil with the herbs, setting away the rest for another time. A beechen bowl was filled with warm water that their guests might wash. While all was doing they beguiled the time with conversation. On the bench designed for the guests was laid a cushion stuffed with seaweed; and a cloth, only produced on great occasions, but old and coarse enough, was spread over that. The old woman, with her apron on, with trembling hand set the table. One leg was shorter than the rest, but a shell put under restored the level. When fixed, she rubbed the table down with some sweet-smelling herbs. Upon it she set some olives, Minerva's fruit, some cornel-berries preserved in vinegar, and added radishes and cheese, with eggs lightly cooked in the ashes. All were served in earthen dishes, and an earthenware pitcher, with wooden cups, stood beside them. When all was ready, the stew, smoking hot, was set on the table. Some wine, not of the oldest, was added; and

for dessert, apples and wild honey; and over and above all, friendly faces, and a simple but hearty welcome.

Now while the repast proceeded, the old folks were astonished to see that the wine, as fast as it was poured out, renewed itself in the pitcher, of its own accord. Struck with terror, Baucis and Philemon recognized their heavenly guests, fell on their knees, and with clasped hands implored forgiveness for their poor entertainment. There was an old goose, which they kept as the guardian of their humble cottage; and they bethought them to make this a sacrifice in honor of their guests. But the goose, too nimble for the old folks, eluded their pursuit with the aid of feet and wings, and at last took shelter between the gods themselves. They forbade it to be slain; and spoke in these words: "We are gods. This inhospitable village shall pay the penalty of its impiety; you alone shall go free from the chastisement. Quit your house, and come with us to the top of yonder hill." They hastened to obey, and staffs in hand, labored up the steep ascent. They had come within an arrow's flight of the top, when turning their eyes below, they beheld all the country sunk in a lake, only their own house left standing. While they gazed with wonder at the sight, and lamented the fate of their neighbors, that old house of theirs was changed into a temple. Columns took the place of the corner-posts, the thatch grew yellow and appeared a gilded roof, the floors became marble, the doors were enriched with carving and ornaments of gold. Then spoke Jupiter in benignant accents: "Excellent old man, and woman worthy of such a husband, speak, tell us your wishes; what favor have you to ask of us?" Philemon took counsel with Baucis a few moments; then declared to the gods their united wish. "We ask to be priests and guardians of this your temple; and since here we have passed our lives in love and concord, we wish that one and the same hour may take us both from life, that I may not live to see her grave, nor be laid in my own by her." Their prayer was granted. They were the keepers of the temple as long as they lived. When grown very old, as they stood one day before the steps of the sacred edifice and were telling the story of the place, Baucis saw Philemon begin to put forth leaves, and old Philemon saw Baucis changing in like manner. And now a leafy crown had grown over their heads, while exchanging parting words, as long as they could speak. "Farewell, dear spouse," they said, together, and at the same moment the bark closed over their mouths. The Tyanean shepherd long showed the two trees, standing side by side, made out of the two good old people.

PLUTO AND PROSERPINE

Under the island of Aetna lies Typhoeus the Titan, in punishment for his share in the rebellion of the giants against Jupiter. Two mountains press down, the one his right and the other his left hand, while Aetna lies over his head. As Typhoeus moves, the earth shakes; as he breathes, smoke and ashes come up from Aetna. Pluto is terrified at the rocking of the earth and fears that his kingdom will be laid open to the light of day. He mounts his chariot with the four black horses and comes up to earth and looks around. While he is thus engaged, Venus, sitting on Mount Eryx playing with her boy Cupid, sees him and says: "My son, take your darts with which you conquer all, even Jove himself, and send one into the breast of yonder dark monarch, who rules the realm of Tartarus. Why should he alone escape? Seize the opportunity to extend your empire and mine. Do you not see that even in heaven some despise our power? Minerva the wise, and Diana the huntress, defy us; and there is that daughter of Ceres, who threatens to follow their example. Now do you, if you have any regard for your own interest or mine, join these two in one." The boy unbound his quiver, and selected his sharpest and truest arrow; then, straining the bow against his knee, he attached the string, and, having made ready, shot the arrow with its barbed point right into the heart of Pluto. In the vale of Enna there is a lake embowered in woods, which screen it from the fervid rays of the sun, while the moist ground is covered with flowers, and spring reigns perpetual. Here Proserpine was playing with her companions, gathering lilies and violets, and filling her basket and her apron with them, when Pluto saw her from his chariot, loved her, and carried her off. She screamed for help to her mother and her companions; and when in her fright she dropped the corners of her apron and let the flowers fall, childlike, she felt the loss of them as an addition to her grief. The ravisher urged on his steeds, calling them each by name, and throwing loose over their heads and necks his iron-colored reins. When he reached the River Cyane, and it opposed his passage, he struck the riverbank with his trident, and the earth opened and gave him a passage to Tartarus.

Ceres sought her daughter all the world over. Bright-haired Aurora, when she came forth in the morning, and Hesperus, when he led out the stars in the evening, found her still busy in the search. But it was all unavailing. At length, weary and sad, she sat down upon a stone and continued sitting nine days and nights, in the open air, under the sunlight and moonlight and falling showers. It was where now stands the city of Eleusis, then the home of an old man named Celeus. He was out in the field, gathering acorns and blackberries, and sticks for his fire. His little girl was driving home their two goats, and as she passed the goddess, who appeared in the guise of an old woman, she said to her, "Mother," and the name was sweet to the ears of Ceres, "why do you sit here alone upon the rocks?" The old man also stopped, though his load was heavy, and begged her to come into his cottage, such as it was. She declined, and he urged her. "Go in peace," she replied, "and be happy in your daughter; I have lost mine." As she spoke, tears, or something like tears, for the gods never weep, fell down her cheeks upon her bosom. The compassionate old man and his child wept with her. Then said he, "Come with us, and despise not our humble roof; so may your daughter be restored to you in safety." "Lead on," said she, "I cannot resist that appeal!" So she rose from the stone and went with them. As they walked he told her that his only son, a little boy, lay very sick, feverish and sleepless. She stooped and gathered some poppies. As they entered the cottage they found all in great distress, for the boy seemed past hope of recovery. Metanira, his mother, received her kindly, and the goddess stooped and kissed the lips of the sick child. Instantly the paleness left his face, and healthy vigor returned to his body. The whole family were delighted, that is, the father, mother, and little girl, for they were all; they had no servants. They spread the table and put upon it curds and cream, apples, and honey in the comb. While they ate, Ceres mingled poppy juice in the milk of the boy. When night came and all was still, she arose, and taking the sleeping boy, molded his limbs with her hands, and uttered over him three times a solemn charm, then went and laid him in the ashes. His mother, who had been watching what her guest was doing, sprang forward with a cry and snatched the child from the fire. Then Ceres assumed her own form, and a divine splendor shone all around. While they were overcome with astonishment, she said, "Mother, you have been cruel in your fondness to your son. I would have made him immortal, but you have frustrated my attempt. Nevertheless, he shall be great and useful. He shall teach men the use of the plow, and the rewards which labor can win from the cultivated soil." So saying, she wrapped a cloud about her, and mounting her chariot rode away.

Ceres continued her search for her daughter, passing from land to land, and across seas and rivers, until at length she returned to Sicily, whence she at first set out, and stood by the banks of the River Cyane, where Pluto made himself a passage with his prize to his own dominions. The river-nymph would have told the goddess all she had witnessed, but dared not, for fear of Pluto; so she only ventured to take up the girdle that Proserpine had dropped in her flight, and waft it to the feet of the mother. Ceres, seeing this, was no longer in doubt of her loss, but she did not yet know the cause, and laid the blame on the innocent land. "Ungrateful soil," said she, "which I have endowed with fertility and clothed with herbage and nourishing grain, No more shall you enjoy my favors" Then the cattle died, the plow broke in the furrow, the seed failed to come up; there was too much sun, there was too much rain; the birds stole the seeds, thistles and brambles were the only growth. Seeing this, the fountain Arethusa interceded for the land. "Goddess," said she, "blame not the land; it opened unwillingly to yield a passage to your daughter. I can tell you of her fate, for I have seen her. This is not my native country; I came hither from Elis. I was a woodland nymph, and delighted in the chase. They praised my beauty, but I cared nothing for it, and rather boasted of my hunting exploits. One day I was returning from the wood, heated with exercise, when I came to a stream silently flowing, so clear that you might count the pebbles on the bottom. The willows shaded it, and the grassy bank sloped down to the water's edge. I approached, I touched the water with my foot. I stepped in knee-deep, and not content with that, I laid my garments on the willows and went in. While I sported in the water, I heard an indistinct murmur coming up as out of the depths of the stream; and made haste to escape to the nearest bank. The voice said, 'Why do you fly, Arethusa? I am Alpheus, the god of this stream.' I ran, he pursued; he was not more swift than I, but he was stronger, and gained upon me, as my strength failed. At last, exhausted, I cried for help to Diana. 'Help me, goddess! Help your votary!' The goddess heard, and wrapped me suddenly in a thick cloud. The river-god looked now this way and now that, and twice came close to me, but could not find me. 'Arethusa! Arethusa!' he cried. Oh, how I trembled, like a lamb that hears the wolf growling outside the fold. A cold sweat came over me, my hair flowed down in streams; where my foot stood there was a pool. In short, in less time than it takes to tell it I became a fountain. But in this form Alpheus knew me, and attempted to mingle his stream with mine. Diana cleft the ground, and I, endeavoring to escape him, plunged into the cavern, and through the bowels of the earth came out here in Sicily. While I passed through the lower parts of the earth, I saw your Proserpine. She was sad, but no longer showing alarm in her countenance. Her look was such as became a queen, the queen of Erebus; the powerful bride of the monarch of the realms of the dead."

When Ceres heard this, she stood for a while like one stupefied; then turned her chariot towards heaven, and hastened to present herself before the throne of Jove. She told the story of her bereavement, and implored Jupiter to interfere to procure the restitution of her daughter. Jupiter consented on one condition, namely, that Proserpine should not during her stay in the lower world have taken any food; otherwise, the Fates forbade her release. Accordingly, Mercury was sent, accompanied by Spring, to demand Proserpine of Pluto. The wily monarch consented; but alas! the maiden had taken a pomegranate which Pluto offered her, and had sucked the sweet pulp from a few of the seeds. This was enough to prevent her complete release; but a compromise was made, by which she was to pass half the time with her mother, and the rest with her husband Pluto. Ceres allowed herself to be pacified with this arrangement, and restored the earth to her favor.

Now she remembered Celeus and his family, and her promise to his infant son Triptolemus. When the boy grew up, she taught him the use of the plow, and how to sow the seed. She took him in her chariot, drawn by winged dragons, through all the countries of the earth, imparting to mankind valuable grains, and the knowledge of agriculture. After his return, Triptolemus built a magnificent temple to Ceres in Eleusis and established the worship of the goddess, under the name of the Eleusinian mysteries, which, in the splendor and solemnity of their observance, surpassed all other religious celebrations among the Greeks. There can be little doubt but that this story of Ceres and Proserpine is an allegory. Proserpine signifies the seed-corn, which, when cast into the ground, lies there concealed, that is, she is carried off by the god of the underworld; when it reappears, Proserpine is restored to her mother. Spring leads her back to the light of day.

The River Alpheus does in fact disappear under ground, in part of its course, finding its way through subterranean channels, until it again appears on the surface. It was said that the Sicilian fountain Arethusa was the same stream, which, after passing under the sea, came up again in Sicily. Hence the story ran that a cup thrown into the Alpheus appeared again in Arethusa.

GLAUCUS AND SCYLLA

Glaucus was a fisherman. One day he had drawn his nets to land and had taken a great many fishes of various kinds. So he emptied his net, and proceeded to sort the fishes on the grass. The place where he stood was a beautiful island in the river, a solitary spot, uninhabited, and not used for pasturage of cattle, nor ever visited by any but himself. On a sudden, the fishes, which had been laid on the grass, began to revive and move their fins as if they were in the water; and while he looked on astonished, they one and all moved off to the water, plunged in and swam away. He did not know what to make of this, whether some god had done it, or some secret power in the herbage. "What herb has such a power?" he exclaimed; and gathering some, he tasted it. Scarce had the juices of the plant reached his palate when he found himself agitated with a longing desire for the water. He could no longer restrain himself, but bidding farewell to earth, he plunged into the stream. The gods of the water received him graciously and admitted him to the honor of their society. They obtained the consent of Oceanus and Tethys, the sovereigns of the sea, that all that was mortal in him should be washed away. A hundred rivers poured their waters over him. Then he lost all sense of his former nature and all consciousness. When he recovered, he found himself changed in form and mind. His hair was sea green and trailed behind him on the water; his shoulders grew broad, and what had been thighs and legs assumed the form of a fish's tail. The sea gods complimented him on the change of his appearance, and he himself was pleased with his looks. One day Glaucus saw the beautiful maiden Scylla, the favorite of the water-nymphs, rambling on the shore, and when she had found a sheltered nook, laving her limbs in the clear water. He fell in love with her, and showing himself on the surface, spoke to her, saying such things as he thought most likely to win her to stay; for she turned to run immediately on sight of him and ran until she had gained a cliff overlooking the sea. Here she stopped and turned round to see whether it was a god or a sea animal, and observed with wonder his shape and color. Glaucus, partly emerging from the water, and supporting himself against a rock, said, "Maiden, I am no monster, nor a sea-animal, but a god; and neither Proteus nor Triton ranks higher than I. Once I was a mortal and followed the sea for a living; but now I belong wholly to it." Then he told the story of his metamorphosis and how he had been promoted to his present dignity, and added, "But what avails all this if it fails to move your heart?" He was going on in this strain, but Scylla turned and hastened away.

Glaucus was in despair, but it occurred to him to consult the enchantress, Circe. Accordingly he repaired to her island, the same where afterwards Ulysses landed, as we shall see in another story. After mutual salutations, he said, "Goddess, I entreat your pity; you alone can relieve the pain I suffer. The power of herbs I know as well as any one, for it is to them I owe my change of form. I love Scylla. I am ashamed to tell you how I have sued and promised to her, and how scornfully she has treated me. I beseech you to use your incantations, or potent herbs, if they are more prevailing, not to cure me of my love, for that I do not wish, but to make her share it and yield me a like return." To which Circe replied, for she was not insensible to the attractions of the sea-green deity, "You had better pursue a willing object; you are worthy to be sought, instead of having to seek in vain. Be not diffident, know your own worth. I protest to you that even I, goddess though I be, and learned in the virtues of plants and spells, should not know how to refuse you. If she scorns you, scorn her; meet one who is ready to meet you halfway, and thus make a due return to both at once." To these words Glaucus replied, "Sooner shall trees grow at the bottom of the ocean, and seaweed on the top of the mountains, than I will cease to love Scylla, and her alone." The goddess was indignant, but she could not punish him, neither did she wish to do so, for she liked him too well; so she turned all her wrath against her rival, poor Scylla. She took plants of poisonous powers and mixed them together, with incantations and charms. Then she passed through the crowd of gamboling beasts, the victims of her art, and proceeded to the coast of Sicily, where Scylla lived. There was a little bay on the shore to which Scylla used to resort, in the heat of the day, to breathe the air of the sea, and to bathe in its waters. Here the goddess poured her poisonous mixture, and muttered over it incantations of mighty power. Scylla came as usual and plunged into the water up to her waist. What was her horror to perceive a brood of serpents and barking monsters surrounding her! At first she could not imagine they were a part of herself, and tried to run from them, and to drive them away; but as she ran she carried them with her, and when she tried to touch her limbs, she found her hands touch only the yawning jaws of monsters. Scylla remained rooted to the spot. Her temper grew as ugly as her form, and she took pleasure in devouring hapless mariners who came within her grasp. Thus she destroyed six of the companions of Ulysses, and tried to wreck the ships of Aeneas, until at last she was turned into a rock, and as such still continues to be a terror to mariners.

CHAPTER V: PYGMALION. VENUS AND ADONIS. APOLLO AND HYACINTHUS. CEYX AND HALCYONE.

PYGMALION

Pygmalion saw so much to blame in women that he came at last to abhor the sex and resolved to live unmarried. He was a sculptor and had made with wonderful skill a statue of ivory, so beautiful that no living woman could be compared to it in beauty. It was indeed the perfect semblance of a maiden that seemed to be alive, and only prevented from moving by modesty. His art was so perfect that it concealed itself, and its product looked like the workmanship of nature. Pygmalion admired his own work and at last fell in love with the counterfeit creation. Oftentimes he laid his hand upon it, as if to assure himself whether it were living or not and could not even then believe that it was only ivory.

Jean-Baptiste Regnault, *Pygmalion Praying to Venus to Animate His Statue,* **1786, oil on Canvas, Salon des Nobles, Chateau de Versailles**

He caressed it and gave it presents such as young girls love: bright shells and polished stones, little birds and flowers of various hues, beads and amber. He put raiment on its limbs, and jewels on its fingers, and a necklace about its neck. To the ears he hung earrings and strings of pearls upon the breast. Her dress became her, and she looked not less charming than when unattired. He laid her on a couch spread with cloths of Tyrian dye, and called her his wife, and put her head upon a pillow of the softest feathers, as if she could enjoy their softness. The festival of Venus was at hand, a festival celebrated with great pomp at Cyprus. Victims were offered, the altars smoked, and the odor of incense filled the air. When Pygmalion had performed his part in the solemnities, he stood before the altar and timidly said, "Ye gods, who can do all things, give me, I pray you, for my wife" he dared not say "my ivory virgin," but said instead "one like my ivory virgin." Venus, who was present at the festival, heard him and knew the thought he would have uttered; and, as an omen of her favor, caused the flame on the altar to shoot up thrice in a fiery point into the air. When he returned home, he went to see his statue, and, leaning over the couch, gave a kiss to the mouth. It seemed to be warm. He pressed its lips again, he laid his hand upon the limbs; the ivory felt soft to his touch, and yielded to his fingers like the wax of Hymettus. While he stands astonished and glad, though doubting, and fears he may be mistaken, again and again with a lover's ardor he touches the object of his hopes. It was indeed alive! The veins when pressed yielded to the finger and then resumed their roundness. Then at last the votary of Venus found words to thank the goddess, and pressed his lips upon lips as real as his own. The virgin felt the kisses and blushed, and, opening her timid eyes to the light, fixed them at the same moment

Laurent de la Hyre, *The Death of Adonis*, c. 1620, Louvre Museum, Paris

on her lover. Venus blessed the nuptials she had formed, and from this union Paphos was born, from whom the city, sacred to Venus, received its name.

VENUS AND ADONIS

Venus, playing one day with her boy Cupid, wounded her bosom with one of his arrows. She pushed him away, but the wound was deeper than she thought. Before it healed she beheld Adonis, and was captivated with him. She no longer took any interest in her favorite resorts, Paphos, and Cnidos, and Amathos, rich in metals. She absented herself even from Olympus, for Adonis was dearer to her than heaven. Him she followed and bore him company. She who used to love to recline in the shade, with no care but to cultivate her charms, now rambled through the woods and over the hills, dressed like the huntress Diana. She called her dogs, and chased hares and stags, or other game that it is safe to hunt, but kept clear of the wolves and bears, reeking with the slaughter of the herd. She charged Adonis, too, to beware of such dangerous animals. "Be brave towards the timid," said she; "courage against the courageous is not safe. Beware how you expose yourself to danger, and put my happiness to risk. Attack not the beasts that Nature has armed with weapons. I do not value your glory so highly as to consent to purchase it by such exposure. Your youth, and the beauty that charms Venus, will not touch the hearts of lions and bristly boars. Think of their terrible claws and prodigious strength! I hate the whole race of them. Do you ask why?" Then she told him the story of Atalanta and Hippomenes, who were changed into lions for their ingratitude to her. Having given him this warning, she mounted her chariot drawn by swans, and drove away through the air. But Adonis was too noble to heed such counsels. The dogs had roused a wild boar from his lair, and the youth threw his spear and wounded the animal with a sidelong stroke. The beast drew out the weapon with his jaws, and rushed after Adonis, who turned and ran; but the boar overtook him, and buried his tusks in his side, and stretched him dying upon the plain. Venus, in her swan-drawn chariot, had not yet reached Cyprus, when she heard coming up through mid air the groans of her beloved, and turned her white-winged coursers back to earth. As she drew near and saw from on high his lifeless body bathed in blood, she alighted, and bending over it beat her breast and tore her hair. Reproaching the Fates, she said, "Yet theirs shall be but a partial triumph; memorials of my grief shall endure, and the spectacle of your death, my Adonis, and of my lamentation shall be annually renewed. Your blood shall be changed into a flower; that consolation none can envy me." Thus speaking, she sprinkled nectar on the blood; and as they mingled, bubbles rose as in a pool on which raindrops fall, and in an hour's time there sprang up a flower of bloody hue like that of a pomegranate. But it is short-lived. It is said the wind blows the blossoms open, and afterwards blows the petals away; so it is called Anemone, or wind Flower, from the cause which assists equally in its production and its decay.

APOLLO AND HYACINTHUS

Apollo was passionately fond of a youth named Hyacinthus. He accompanied him in his sports, carried the nets when he went fishing, led the dogs when he went to hunt, followed him in his excursions in the mountains, and neglected for him his lyre and his arrows. One day they played a game of quoits together, and Apollo, heaving aloft the discus, with strength mingled with skill, sent it high and far. Hyacinthus watched it as it flew, and excited with the sport ran forward to seize it, eager to make his throw, when the quoit bounded from the earth and struck him in the forehead. He fainted and fell. The god, as pale as himself, raised him and tried all his art to stanch the wound and retain the flitting life, but all in vain; the hurt was past the power of medicine. As, when one has broken the stem of a lily in the garden, it hangs its head and turns its flowers to the earth, so the head of the dying boy, as if too heavy for his neck, fell over on his shoulder. "Thou diest, Hyacinth," so spoke Phoebus, "robbed of thy youth by me. Thine is the suffering, mine the crime. Would that I could die for thee! But since that may not be thou shalt live with me in memory and in song. My lyre shall celebrate thee, my song shall tell thy fate, and thou shalt become a flower inscribed with my regrets." While Apollo spoke, behold the blood which had flowed on the ground and stained the herbage, ceased to be blood; but a flower of hue more beautiful than the Tyrian sprang up, resembling the lily, if it were not that this is purple and that silvery white (it is evidently not our modern hyacinth that is here described. It is perhaps some species of iris, or perhaps of larkspur, or of pansy.) And this was not enough for Phoebus; but to confer still greater honor, he marked the petals with his sorrow, and inscribed "Ah! Ah!" upon them, as we see to this day. The flower bears the name of Hyacinthus, and with every returning spring revives the memory of his fate. It was said that Zephyrus (the West Wind), who was also fond of Hyacinthus and jealous of his preference of Apollo, blew the quoit out of its course to make it strike Hyacinthus.

CEYX AND HALCYONE

Ceyx was King of Thessaly, where he reigned in peace without violence or wrong. He was son of Hesperus, the day star, and the glow of his beauty reminded one of his father. Halcyone, the daughter of Aeolus, was his wife and devotedly attached to him. Now Ceyx was in deep affliction for the loss of his brother, and direful prodigies following his brother's death made him feel as if the gods were hostile to him. He thought best therefore to make a voyage to Claros in Ionia, to consult the oracle of Apollo. But as soon as he disclosed his intention to his wife Halcyone, a shudder ran through her frame, and her face grew deadly pale. "What fault of mine, dearest husband, has turned your affection from me? Where is that love of me that used to be uppermost in your thoughts? Have you learned to feel easy in the absence of Halcyone? Would you rather have me away?" She also endeavored to discourage him, by describing the violence of the winds, which she had known familiarly when she lived at home in her father's house, Aeolus being the god of the winds, and having as much as he could do to restrain them. "They rush together," said she, "with such fury that fire flashes from the conflict. But if you must go," she added, "dear husband, let me go with you, Otherwise I shall suffer, not only the real evils which you must encounter, but those also which my fears suggest." These words weighed heavily on the mind of king Ceyx, and it was no less his own wish than hers to take her with him, but he could not bear to expose her to the dangers of the sea. He answered, therefore, consoling her as well as he could, and finished with these words: "I promise, by the rays of my father the Day-star, that if fate permits I will return before the moon shall have twice rounded her orb." When he had thus spoken he ordered the vessel to be drawn out of the ship house, and the oars and sails to be put aboard. When Halcyone saw these preparations she shuddered, as if with a presentiment of evil. With tears and sobs she said farewell, and then fell senseless to the ground.

Meanwhile, Ceyx and his men glide out of the harbor, and the breeze plays among the ropes. The seamen draw in their oars, and hoist their sails. When half or less of their course was passed, as night drew on, the sea began to whiten with swelling waves, and the east wind to blow a gale. The master gives the word to take in sail, but the storm forbids obedience, for such is the roar of the winds and waves that his orders are unheard. The men, of their own accord, busy themselves to secure the oars, to strengthen the ship, to reef the sail. While they thus do what to each one seems best, the storm increases. The shouting of the men, the rattling of the shrouds, and the dashing of the waves, mingle with the roar of the thunder. The swelling sea seems lifted up to the heavens, to scatter its foam among the clouds; then sinking away to the bottom assumes the color of the shoal, a Stygian blackness. The vessel obeys all these changes. It seems like a wild beast that rushes on the spears of the hunters. Rain falls in torrents, as if the skies were coming down to unite with the sea. When the lightning ceases for a moment, the night seems to add its own darkness to that of the storm; then comes the flash, rending the darkness asunder, and lighting up all with a glare. Skill fails, courage sinks, and death seems to come on every wave. The men are stupefied with terror. The thought of parents, and kindred, and pledges left at home, comes over their minds. Ceyx thinks of Halcyone. No name but hers is on his lips, and while he yearns for her, he yet rejoices in her absence. Presently the mast is shattered by a stroke of lightning, the rudder broken, and the triumphant surge curling

over looks down upon the wreck, then falls, and crushes it to fragments. Some of the seamen, stunned by the stroke, sink, and rise no more; others cling to fragments of the wreck. Ceyx, with the hand that used to grasp the scepter, holds fast to a plank, calling for help, alas, in vain, upon his father and his father-in-law. But oftenest on his lips was the name of Halcyone. His thoughts cling to her. He prays that the waves may bear his body to her sight, and that it may receive burial at her hands. At length the waters overwhelm him, and he sinks. The day star looked dim that night. Since it could not leave the heavens, it shrouded its face with clouds. In the meanwhile Halcyone, ignorant of all these horrors, counted the days until her husband's promised return. Now she gets ready the garments that he shall put on, and now what she shall wear when he arrives. To all the gods she offers frequent incense but more than all to Juno. For her husband, who was no more, she prayed incessantly; that he might be safe; that he might come home; that he might not, in his absence, see any one that he would love better than her. But of all these prayers, the last was the only one destined to be granted. The goddess, at length, could not bear any longer to be pleaded with for one already dead, and to have hands raised to her altars, that ought rather to be offering funeral rites. So, calling Iris, she said, "Iris, my faithful messenger, go to the drowsy dwelling of Somnus, and tell him to send a vision to Halcyone, in the form of Ceyx, to make known to her the event."

Iris puts on her robe of many colors, and tingeing the sky with her bow, seeks the palace of the King of Sleep. Near the Cimmerian country, a mountain cave is the abode of the dull god, Somnus, Here Phoebus dares not come, either rising, or at midday, or setting. Clouds and shadows are exhaled from the ground, and the light glimmers faintly. The bird of dawn, with crested head, never calls aloud there to Aurora, nor watchful dog, nor more sagacious goose disturbs the silence. No wild beast, nor cattle, nor branch moved with the wind, nor sound of human conversation, breaks the stillness. Silence reigns there; and from the bottom of the rock the River Lethe flows, and by its murmur invites to sleep. Poppies grow abundantly before the door of the cave, and other herbs, from whose juices Night collects slumbers, which she scatters over the darkened earth. There is no gate to the mansion, to creak on its hinges, nor any watchman; but in the midst, a couch of black ebony, adorned with black plumes and black curtains. There the god reclines, his limbs relaxed with sleep. Around him lie dreams, resembling all various forms, as many as the harvest bears stalks, or the forest leaves, or the seashore grains of sand. As soon as the goddess entered and brushed away the dreams that hovered around her, her brightness lit up all the cave. The god, scarce opening his eyes, and ever and anon dropping his beard upon his breast, at last shook himself free from himself, and leaning on his arm, inquired her errand, for he knew who she was. She answered, "Somnus, gentlest of the gods, tranquillizer of minds and soother of careworn hearts, Juno sends you her commands that you dispatch a dream to Halcyone, in the city of Trachinae, representing her lost husband and all the events of the wreck." Having delivered her message, Iris hasted away, for she could not longer endure the stagnant air, and as she felt drowsiness creeping over her, she made her escape, and returned by her bow the way she came. Then Somnus called one of his numerous sons, Morpheus, the most expert at counterfeiting forms, and in imitating the walk, the countenance, and mode of speaking, even the clothes and attitudes most characteristic of each. But he only imitates men, leaving it to another to personate birds, beasts, and serpents. Him they call Icelos;

René-Antoine Houasse, *Morpheus Awakens as Iris Draws Near,* 1690, Palace of Versailles

and Phantasos is a third, who turns himself into rocks, waters, woods, and other things without life. These wait upon kings and great personages in their sleeping hours, while others move among the common people. Somnus chose, from all the brothers, Morpheus, to perform the command of Iris; then laid his head on his pillow and yielded himself to grateful repose. Morpheus flew, making no noise with his wings, and soon came to the Haemonian city, where, laying aside his wings, he assumed the form of Ceyx.

43

Under that form, but pale like a dead man, naked, he stood before the couch of the wretched wife. His beard seemed soaked with water, and water trickled from his drowned locks. Leaning over the bed, tears streaming from his eyes, he said, "Do you recognize your Ceyx, unhappy wife, or has death too much changed my visage? Behold me, know me, your husband's shade, instead of himself. Your prayers, Halcyone, availed me nothing. I am dead. No more deceive yourself with vain hopes of my return. The stormy winds sunk my ship in the Aegean Sea; waves filled my mouth while it called aloud on you. No uncertain messenger tells you this, no vague rumor brings it to your ears. I come in person, a shipwrecked man, to tell you my fate. Arise! Give me tears, give me lamentations, let me not go down to Tartarus unwept." To these words Morpheus added the voice that seemed to be that of her husband; he seemed to pour forth genuine tears; his hands had the gestures of Ceyx. Halcyone, weeping, groaned, and stretched out her arms in her sleep, striving to embrace his body, but grasping only the air. "Stay!" she cried; "whither do you fly? Let us go together." Her own voice awakened her. Starting up, she gazed eagerly around, to see if he was still present, for the servants, alarmed by her cries, had brought a light. When she found him not, she smote her breast and rent her garments. She cares not to unbind her hair, but tears it wildly. Her nurse asks what is the cause of her grief. "Halcyone is no more," she answers; "she perished with her Ceyx. Utter not words of comfort, he is shipwrecked and dead. I have seen him. I have recognized him. I stretched out my hands to seize him and detain him. His shade vanished, but it was the true shade of my husband. Not with the accustomed features, not with the beauty that was his, but pale, naked, and with his hair wet with seawater, he appeared to wretched me. Here, in this very spot, the sad vision stood," and she looked to find the mark of his footsteps. "This it was, this that my presaging mind foreboded, when I implored him not to leave me to trust himself to the waves. O, how I wish, since thou wouldst go, that thou hadst taken me with thee! It would have been far better. Then I should have had no remnant of life to spend without thee, nor a separate death to die. If I could bear to live and struggle to endure, I should be more cruel to myself

than the sea has been to me. But I will not struggle. I will not be separated from thee, unhappy husband. This time, at least I will keep thee company. In death, if one tomb may not include us, one epitaph shall; if I may not lay my ashes with thine, my name, at least, shall not be separated." Her grief forbade more words, and these were broken with tears and sobs. It was now morning. She went to the seashore and sought the spot where she last saw him, on his departure. "Here he lingered and cast off his tacklings and gave me his last kiss." While she reviews every moment, and strives to recall every incident, looking out over the sea, she descries an indistinct object floating in the water. At first she was in doubt what it was, but by degrees the waves bore it nearer, and it was plainly the body of a man. Though unknowing of whom, yet, as it was of some shipwrecked one, she was deeply moved, and gave it her tears, saying, "Alas! Unhappy one, and unhappy, if such there be, thy wife!" Borne by the waves, it came nearer. As she more and more nearly views it, she trembles more and more. Now, now it approaches the shore. Now marks that she recognizes appear. It is her husband! Stretching out her trembling hands towards it, she exclaims, "O, dearest husband, is it thus you return to me?" There was built out from the shore a mole, constructed to break the assaults of the sea, and stem its violent ingress. She leaped upon this barrier and (it was wonderful she could do so) she flew, and striking the air with wings produced on the instant, skimmed along the surface of the water, an unhappy bird. As she flew, her throat poured forth sounds full of grief, and like the voice of one lamenting. When she touched the mute and bloodless body, she enfolded its beloved limbs with her new-formed wings, and tried to give kisses with her horny beak. Whether Ceyx felt it, or whether it was only the action of the waves, those who looked on doubted, but the body seemed to raise its head. But indeed he did feel it, and by the pitying gods both of them were changed into birds. They mate and have their young ones. For seven placid days, in winter time, Halcyone broods over her nest, which floats upon the sea. Then the way is safe to seamen. Aeolus guards the winds and keeps them from disturbing the deep. The sea is given up, for the time, to his grandchildren.

CHAPTER VI: VERTUMNUS AND POMONA. CUPID AND PSYCHE.

VERTUMNUS AND POMONA

The Hamadryads were Wood nymphs. Among them was Pomona, and no one excelled her in love of the garden and the culture of fruit. She cared not for forests and rivers but loved the cultivated country and trees that bear delicious apples. Her right hand bore for its weapon not a javelin, but a pruning knife. Armed with this, she worked at one time, to repress the too luxuriant growths, and curtail the branches that straggled out of place; at another, to split the twig and insert therein a graft, making the branch adopt a nursling not its own. She took care, too, that her favorites should not suffer from drought and led streams of water by them that the thirsty roots might drink. This occupation was her pursuit, her passion, and she was free from that which Venus inspires. She was not without fear of the country people, and kept her orchard locked, and allowed not men to enter. The Fauns and Satyrs would have given all they possessed to win her, and so would old Sylvanus, who looks young for his years, and Pan, who wears a garland of pine leaves around his head. But Vertumnus loved her best of all; yet he sped no better than the rest. Oh, how often, in the disguise of a reaper, did he bring her corn in a basket, looking the very image of a reaper! With a hay-band tied round him, one would think he had just come from turning over the grass. Sometimes he would have an ox-goad in his hand, and you would have said he had just unyoked his weary oxen. Now he bore a pruning hook and personated a vinedresser; and again with a ladder on his shoulder, he seemed as if he was going to gather apples. Sometimes he trudged along as a discharged soldier, and again he bore a fishing rod as if going to fish. In this way, he gained admission to her, again and again, and fed his passion with the sight of her.

One day he came in the guise of an old woman, her gray hair surmounted with a cap, and a staff in her hand. She entered the garden and admired the fruit. "It does you credit, my dear," she said, and kissed Pomona, not exactly with an old woman's kiss. She sat down on a bank, and looked up at the branches laden with fruit that hung over her. Opposite was an elm entwined with a vine loaded with swelling grapes. She praised the tree and its associated vine, equally. "But," said Vertumnus, "if the tree stood alone and had no vine clinging to it, it would lie prostrate on the ground. Why will you not

Ferdinand Bol, *Vertumnus and Pomona*, 1644, oil on canvas, Cincinnati Museum of Art (Photograph © Wmpearl)

take a lesson from the tree and the vine, and consent to unite yourself with some one? I wish you would. Helen herself had not more numerous suitors, nor Penelope, the wife of shrewd Ulysses. Even while you spurn them, they court you — rural deities and others of every kind that frequent these mountains. But if you are prudent and want to make a good alliance, and will let an old woman advise you, who loves you better than you have any idea of, dismiss all the rest and accept Vertumnus, on my recommendation. I know him as well as he knows himself. He is not a wandering deity but belongs to these mountains. Nor is he like too many of the lovers nowadays, who love any one they happen to see; he loves you, and you only. Add to this, he is young and handsome, and has the art of assuming any shape he pleases, and can make himself just what you command him. Moreover, he loves the same things that you do, delights in gardening, and handles your apples with admiration. But now he cares nothing for fruits, nor flowers, nor anything else, but only yourself. Take pity on him, and fancy him speaking now with my mouth. Remember that the gods punish cruelty, and that Venus hates a hard heart, and will visit such offenses sooner or later. To prove this, let me tell you a story, which is well known in Cyprus to be a fact; and I hope it will have the effect to make you more merciful.

"Iphis was a young man of humble parentage, who saw and loved Anaxarete, a noble lady of the ancient family of Teucer. He struggled long with his passion, but when he found he could not subdue it, he came a suppliant to her mansion. First he told his passion to her nurse and begged her as she loved her foster-child to favor his suit. And then he tried to win her domestics to his side. Sometimes he committed his vows to written tablets and often hung at her door garlands that he had moistened with his tears. He stretched himself on her threshold, and uttered his complaints to the cruel bolts and bars. She was deafer than the surges that rise in the November gale; harder than steel from the German forges, or a rock that still clings to its native cliff. She mocked and laughed at him, adding cruel words to her ungentle treatment, and gave

not the slightest gleam of hope. Iphis could not any longer endure the torments of hopeless love, and standing before her doors, he spake these last words: 'Anaxarete, you have conquered and shall no longer have to bear my importunities. Enjoy your triumph! Sing songs of joy and bind your forehead with laurel, you have conquered! I die; stony heart, rejoice! This at least I can do to gratify you and force you to praise me; and thus shall I prove that the love of you left me but with life. Nor will I leave it to rumor to tell you of my death. I will come myself, and you shall see me die, and feast your eyes on the spectacle. Yet, Oh, ye gods, who look down on mortal woes, observe my fate! I ask but this! Let me be remembered in coming ages and add those years to my name which you have taken from my life.' Thus he said, and, turning his pale face and weeping eyes towards her mansion, he fastened a rope to the gatepost, on which he had hung garlands, and putting his head into the noose, he murmured, 'This garland at least will please you, cruel girl!' And falling, hung suspended with his neck broken.

"As he fell he struck against the gate, and the sound was as the sound of a groan. The servants opened the door and found him dead, and with exclamations of pity raised him and carried him home to his mother, for his father was not living. She received the dead body of her son and folded the cold form to her bosom; while she poured forth the sad words that bereaved mothers utter. The mournful funeral passed through the town, and the pale corpse was borne on a bier to the place of the funeral pile. By chance the home of Anaxarete was on the street where the procession passed, and the lamentations of the mourners met the ears of her whom the avenging deity had already marked for punishment. 'Let us see this sad procession,' said she, and mounted to a turret, whence through an open window she looked upon the funeral. Scarce had her eyes rested upon the form of Iphis stretched on the bier, when they began to stiffen, and the warm blood in her body to become cold. Endeavoring to step back, she found she could not move her feet; trying to turn away her face, she tried in vain;

François Gerard, *Cupid and Psyche,* 1798, oil on canvas, Louvre, Paris and by degrees all her limbs became stony like her heart. That you may not doubt the fact, the statue still remains, and stands in the temple of Venus at Salamis, in the exact form of the lady. Now think of these things, my dear, and lay aside your scorn and your delays, and accept a lover. So may neither the vernal frosts blight your young fruits, nor furious winds scatter your blossoms!"

When Vertumnus had spoken thus, he dropped the disguise of an old woman, and stood before her in his proper person, as a comely youth. It appeared to her like the sun bursting through a cloud. He would have renewed his entreaties, but there was no need; his arguments and the sight of his true form prevailed, and the Nymph no longer resisted but owned a mutual flame.

CUPID AND PSYCHE

A certain king had three daughters. The two elder were charming girls, but the beauty of the youngest was so wonderful that language is too poor to express its due praise. The fame of her beauty was so great that strangers from neighboring countries came in crowds to enjoy the sight, and looked on her with amazement, paying her that homage which is due only to Venus herself. In fact, Venus found her altars deserted, while men turned their devotion to this young virgin. As she passed along, the people sang her praises, and strewed her way with chaplets and flowers. This perversion to a mortal of the homage due only to the immortal powers gave great offence to the real Venus. Shaking her ambrosial locks with indignation, she exclaimed, "Am I then to be eclipsed in my honors by a mortal girl? In vain then did that royal shepherd, whose judgment was approved by Jove himself, give me the palm of beauty over my illustrious rivals, Pallas and Juno. But she shall not so quietly usurp my honors. I will give her cause to repent of so unlawful a beauty." Thereupon she calls her winged son Cupid, mischievous enough in his own nature, and rouses and provokes him yet more by her complaints. She points out Psyche to him, and says, "My dear son, punish that contumacious beauty; give thy mother a revenge as sweet as her injuries are great; infuse into the bosom of that haughty girl a passion for some low, mean, unworthy being, so that she may reap a mortification as great as her present exultation and triumph." Cupid prepared to obey the commands of his mother. There are two fountains in Venus's garden, one of sweet waters, the other of bitter. Cupid filled two amber vases, one from each fountain, and suspending them from the top of his quiver, hastened to the chamber of Psyche, whom he found asleep. He shed a few drops from the bitter fountain over her lips, though the sight of her almost moved him to pity; then touched her side with the point of his arrow. At the touch she awoke, and opened eyes upon Cupid (himself invisible), which so startled him that in his confusion he wounded himself with his own arrow. Heedless of his wound his whole thought now was to repair the mischief he had done, and he poured the balmy drops of joy over all her silken ringlets.

Psyche, henceforth frowned upon by Venus, derived no benefit from all her charms. True, all eyes were cast eagerly upon her, and every mouth spoke her praises; but neither king, royal youth, nor plebeian presented himself to demand her in marriage. Her two elder sisters of moderate charms had now long been married to two royal princes; but Psyche, in her lonely apartment, deplored her solitude, sick of that beauty, which, while it procured abundance of flattery, had failed to awaken love. Her parents, afraid that they had unwittingly incurred the anger of the gods, consulted the oracle of Apollo, and received this answer: "The virgin is destined for the bride of no mortal lover. Her future husband awaits her on the top of the mountain. He is a monster whom neither gods nor men can resist." This dreadful decree of the oracle filled all the people with dismay, and her parents abandoned themselves to grief. But Psyche said, "Why, my dear parents, do you now lament me? You should rather have grieved when the people showered upon me undeserved honors, and with one voice called me a Venus. I now perceive that I am a victim to that name. I submit. Lead me to that rock to which my unhappy fate has destined me."

Edward Burne-Jones, *Psyche's Wedding,* **1895, oil on canvas, Royal Museums of Fine Art, Brussels, Belgium**

Accordingly, all things being prepared, the royal maid took her place in the procession, which more resembled a funeral than a nuptial pomp, and with her parents, amid the lamentations of the people, ascended the mountain, on the summit of which they left her alone, and with sorrowful hearts returned home. While Psyche stood on the ridge of the mountain, panting with fear and with eyes full of tears, the gentle Zephyr raised her from the earth and bore her with an easy motion into a flowery dale. By degrees her mind became composed, and she laid herself down on the grassy bank to sleep. When she awoke, refreshed with sleep, she looked round and beheld nearby a pleasant grove of tall and stately trees. She entered it, and in the midst discovered a fountain, sending forth clear and crystal waters, and hard by, a magnificent palace whose august front impressed the spectator that it was not the work of mortal hands, but the happy retreat of some god. Drawn by admiration and wonder, she approached the building and ventured to enter. Every object she met filled her with pleasure and amazement. Golden pillars supported the vaulted roof, and the walls were enriched with carvings and paintings representing beasts of the chase and rural scenes, adapted to delight the eye of the beholder. Proceeding onward she perceived that besides the apartments of state there were others, filled with all manner of treasures and beautiful and precious productions of nature and art. While her eyes were thus occupied, a voice addressed her, though she saw no one, uttering these words: "Sovereign lady, all that you see is yours. We whose voices you hear are your servants, and shall obey all your commands with our utmost care and diligence. Retire therefore to your chamber and repose on your bed of down, and when you see fit repair to the bath. Supper will await you in the adjoining alcove when it pleases you to take your seat there." Psyche gave ear to the admonitions of her vocal attendants, and after repose and the refreshment of the bath, seated herself in the alcove, where a table immediately presented itself, without any visible aid from waiters or servants, and covered with the greatest delicacies of food and the most nectareous wines. Her ears too were feasted with music from invisible performers; of whom one sang, another played on the lute, and all closed in the wonderful harmony of a full chorus. She had not yet seen her destined husband. He came only in the hours of darkness and fled before the dawn of morning, but his accents were full of love and inspired a like passion in her. She often begged him to stay and let her behold him, but he would not consent. On the contrary, he charged her to make no attempt to see him, for it was his pleasure, for the best of reasons, to keep concealed. "Why should you wish to behold me?" he said. "Have you any doubt of my love? Have you any wish ungratified? If you saw me, perhaps you would fear me, perhaps adore me, but all I ask of you is to love me. I would rather you would love me as an equal than adore me as a god." This reasoning somewhat quieted Psyche for a time, and while the novelty lasted she felt quite happy. But at length the thought of her parents, left in ignorance of her fate, and of her sisters, precluded from sharing with her the delights of her situation, preyed on her mind and made her begin to feel her palace as but a splendid prison.

When her husband came one night, she told him her distress, and at last drew from him an unwilling consent that her sisters should be brought to see her. So calling Zephyr, she acquainted him with her husband's commands, and he, promptly obedient, soon brought them across the mountain down to their sister's valley. They embraced her and she returned their caresses. "Come," said Psyche, "enter with me my house and refresh yourselves with whatever your sister has to offer." Then taking their hands she led them into her golden palace and committed them to the care of her numerous train of attendant voices, to refresh them in her baths and at her table, and to show them all her treasures. The view of these celestial delights caused envy to enter their bosoms, at seeing their young sister possessed of such state and splendor, so much exceeding their own. They asked her numberless questions, among others what sort of a person her husband was. Psyche replied that he was a beautiful youth, who generally spent the daytime in hunting upon the mountains. The sisters, not satisfied with this reply, soon made her confess that she had never seen him. Then they proceeded to fill her bosom with dark suspicions. "Call to mind," they said, "the Pythian oracle that declared you destined to marry a direful and tremendous monster. The inhabitants of this valley say that your husband is a terrible and monstrous serpent, who nourishes you for a while with dainties that he may by and by devour you. Take our advice. Provide yourself with a lamp and a sharp knife; put them in concealment that your husband may not discover them, and when he is sound asleep, slip out of bed bring forth your lamp and see for yourself whether what they say is true or not. If it is, hesitate not to cut off the monster's head, and thereby recover your liberty." Psyche resisted these persuasions as well as she could, but they did not fail to have their effect on her mind, and when her sisters were gone, their words and her own curiosity were too strong for her to resist. So she prepared her lamp and a sharp knife, and hid them out of sight of her husband. When he had fallen into his first sleep, she silently rose and uncovering her lamp beheld not a hideous monster, but the most beautiful and charming of the gods, with his golden ringlets wandering over his snowy neck and crimson cheek, with two dewy wings on his shoulders, whiter than snow, and with shining feathers like the tender blossoms of spring. As she leaned the lamp over to have a nearer view of his face a drop of burning oil fell on the shoulder of the god, startled with which he opened his eyes and fixed them full upon her; then, without saying one word, he spread his white wings and flew out of the window. Psyche, in vain endeavoring to follow him, fell from the window to the ground. Cupid, beholding her as she lay in the dust, stopped his flight for an instant and said, "O foolish Psyche, is it thus you repay my love? After having disobeyed my mother's commands and made you my wife, will you think me a monster and cut off my head? But go; return to your sisters, whose advice you seem to think preferable to mine. I inflict no other punishment on you than to leave you forever. Love cannot dwell with suspicion." So saying he fled away, leaving poor Psyche prostrate on the ground, filling the place with mournful lamentations. When she had recovered some degree of composure she looked around her, but the palace and gardens had vanished, and she found herself in the open field not far from the city where her sisters dwelt. She repaired thither and told them the whole story of her misfortunes, at which, pretending to grieve, those spiteful creatures inwardly rejoiced. "For now," said they, "he will perhaps choose one of us."

With this idea, without saying a word of her intentions, each of them rose early the next morning and ascended the mountain, and having reached the top, called upon Zephyr to receive her and bear her to his lord; then leaping up, and not being sustained by Zephyr, fell down the precipice and was dashed to pieces. Psyche meanwhile wandered day and night, without food or repose, in search of her husband. Casting her eyes on a lofty mountain having on its brow a magnificent temple, she sighed and said to herself, "Perhaps my love, my lord, inhabits there," and directed her steps thither. She had no sooner entered than she saw heaps of corn, some in loose ears and some in sheaves, with mingled ears of barley. Scattered about lay sickles and rakes, and all the instruments of harvest, without order, as if thrown carelessly out of the weary reapers' hands in the sultry hours of the day. This unseemly con-

fusion the pious Psyche put an end to, by separating and sorting every thing to its proper place and kind, believing that she ought to neglect none of the gods, but endeavor by her piety to engage them all in her behalf. The holy Ceres, whose temple it was, finding her so religiously employed, thus spoke to her: "O Psyche, truly worthy of our pity, though I cannot shield you from the frowns of Venus, yet I can teach you how best to allay her displeasure. Go then, voluntarily surrender yourself to your lady and sovereign, and try by modesty and submission to win her forgiveness; perhaps her favor will restore you the husband you have lost."

Psyche obeyed the commands of Ceres and took her way to the temple of Venus, endeavoring to fortify her mind and thinking of what she should say and how she should best propitiate the angry goddess, feeling that the issue was doubtful and perhaps fatal. Venus received her with angry countenance. "Most undutiful and faithless of servants," said she, "do you at last remember that you really have a mistress? Or have you rather come to see your sick husband, yet suffering from the wound given him by his loving wife? You are so ill favored and disagreeable that the only way you can merit your lover must be by dint of industry and diligence. I will make trial of your housewifery." Then she ordered Psyche to be led to the storehouse of her temple, where was laid up a great quantity of wheat, barley, millet, vetches, beans, and lentils prepared for food for her doves, and said, "Take and separate all these grains, putting all of the same kind in a parcel by themselves, and see that you get it done before evening." Then Venus departed and left her to her task. But Psyche, in perfect consternation at the enormous work, sat stupid and silent, without moving a finger to the inextricable heap. While she sat despairing, Cupid stirred up the little ant, a native of the fields, to take compassion on her. The leader of the anthill, followed by whole hosts of his six-legged subjects, approached the heap, and with the utmost diligence taking grain by grain, they separated the pile, sorting each kind to its parcel; and when it was all done, they vanished out of sight in a moment. Venus at the approach of twilight returned from the banquet of the gods, breathing odors and crowned with roses. Seeing the task done she exclaimed, "This is no work of yours wicked one, but his, whom to your own and his misfortune you have enticed." So saying, she threw her a piece of black bread for her supper and went away. Next morning Venus ordered Psyche to be called, and said to her, "Behold yonder grove which stretches along the margin of the water. There you will find sheep feeding without a shepherd, with golden-shining fleeces on their backs. Go, fetch me a sample of that precious wool gathered from every one of their fleeces." Psyche obediently went to the riverside, prepared to do her best to execute the command. But the river-god inspired the reeds with harmonious murmurs, which seemed to say, "O maiden, severely tried, tempt not the dangerous flood, nor venture among the formidable rams on the other side, for as long as they are under the influence of the rising sun, they burn with a cruel rage to destroy mortals with their sharp horns or rude teeth. But when the noontide sun has driven the flock to the shade, and the serene spirit of the flood has lulled them to rest, you may then cross in safety, and you will find the woolly gold sticking to the bushes and the trunks of the trees." Thus the compassionate river-god gave Psyche instructions how to accomplish her task, and by observing his directions she soon returned to Venus with her arms full of the golden fleece; but she received not the approbation of her implacable mistress, who said, "I know very well it is by none of your own doings that you have succeeded in this task, and I am not satisfied yet that you have any capacity to make yourself useful. But I have another task for you. Here, take this box, and go your way to the infernal shades, and give this box to Proserpine, and say, 'My mistress Venus desires you to send her a little of your beauty, for in tending her sick son she has lost some of her own.' Be not too long on your errand, for I must paint myself with it to appear at the circle of the gods and goddesses this evening."

Psyche was now satisfied that her destruction was at hand, being obliged to go with her own feet directly down to Erebus. Wherefore, to make no delay of what was not to be avoided, she goes to the top of a high tower to precipitate herself headlong, thus to descend the shortest way to the shades below. But a voice from the tower said to her, "Why, poor unlucky girl, dost thou design to put an end to thy days in so dreadful a manner? And what cowardice makes thee sink under this last danger, who hast been so miraculously supported in all thy former?" Then the voice told her how by a certain cave she might reach the realms of Pluto, and how to avoid all the dangers of the road, to pass by Cerberus, the three-headed dog, and prevail on Charon, the ferryman, to take her across the black river and bring her back again. But the voice added, "When Proserpine has given you the box, filled with her beauty, of all things this is chiefly to be observed by you, that you never once open or look into the box nor allow your curiosity to pry into the treasure of the beauty of the goddesses." Psyche encouraged by this advice obeyed it in all things and taking heed to her ways traveled safely to the kingdom of Pluto. She was admitted to the palace of Proserpine, and without accepting the delicate seat or delicious banquet that was offered her, but contented with coarse bread for her food, she delivered her message from Venus. Presently the box was returned to her, shut and filled with the precious commodity. Then she returned the way she came, and glad was she to come out once more into the light of day. But having got so far successfully through her dangerous task a longing desire seized her to examine the contents of the box. "What," said she, "shall I, the carrier of this divine beauty, not take the least bit to put on my cheeks to appear to more advantage in the eyes of my beloved husband!" So she carefully opened the box, but found nothing there of any beauty at all, but an infernal and truly Stygian sleep, which being thus set free from its prison, took possession of her, and she fell down in the midst of the road, a sleepy corpse without sense or motion. But Cupid being now recovered from his wound, and not able longer to bear the absence of his beloved Psyche, slipping through the smallest crack of the window of his chamber which happened to be left open, flew to the spot where Psyche lay and gathering up the sleep from her body closed it again in the box, and waked Psyche with a light touch of one of his arrows. "Again," said he, "hast thou almost perished by the same curiosity. But now perform exactly the task imposed on you by my mother, and I will take care of the rest." Then Cupid, as swift as lightning penetrating the heights of heaven, presented himself before Jupiter with his supplication. Jupiter lent a favoring ear and pleaded the cause of the lovers so earnestly with Venus that he won her consent. On this he sent Mercury to bring Psyche up to the heavenly assembly, and when she arrived, handing her a cup of ambrosia, he said, "Drink this, Psyche, and be immortal; nor shall Cupid ever break away from the knot in which he is tied, but these nuptials shall be perpetual." Thus Psyche became at last united to Cupid, and in due time they had a daughter born to them whose name was Pleasure.

Orazio Gentileschi, *Cupid and Psyche,* c. 1620, oil on canvas, Hermitage Museum, St. Petersburg, Russia

Erasmus Quellinus, *The Rape of Europa,* 1634, Prado, Madrid

CHAPTER VII: CADMUS. THE MYRMIDONS.

CADMUS

Jupiter, under the disguise of a bull, had carried away to the island of Crete, Europa, the daughter of Agenor king of Phoenicia. Agenor commanded his son Cadmus to go in search of his sister, and not to return without her. Cadmus went and sought long and far for his sister, but could not find her, and not daring to return unsuccessful, consulted the oracle of Apollo to know what country he should settle in. The oracle informed him that he should find a cow in the field, and should follow her wherever she might wander, and where she stopped, should build a city and call it Thebes. Cadmus had hardly left the Castalian cave, from which the oracle was delivered, when he saw a young cow slowly walking before him. He followed her close, offering at the same time his prayers to Phoebus. The cow went on until she passed the shallow channel of Cephisus and came out into the plain of Panope. There she stood still, and raising her broad forehead to the sky, filled the air with her lowings. Cadmus gave thanks, and stooping down kissed the foreign soil, then lifting his eyes, greeted the surrounding mountains. Wishing to offer a sacrifice to Jupiter, he sent his servants to seek pure water for a libation. Nearby there stood an ancient grove which had never been profaned by the axe, in the midst of which was a cave, thick covered with the growth of bushes, its roof forming a low arch, from beneath which burst forth a fountain of purest water. In the cave lurked a horrid serpent with a crested head and scales glittering like gold. His eyes shone like fire, his body was swollen with venom. He vibrated a triple tongue and showed a triple row of teeth. No sooner had the Tyrians (Cadmus and his companions came from Tyre, the chief city of Phoenicia) dipped their pitchers in the fountain, and the thrushing waters made a sound, than the glittering serpent raised his head out of the cave and uttered a fearful hiss. The vessels fell from their hands, the blood left their cheeks, and they trembled in every limb. The serpent, twisting his scaly body in a huge coil, raised his head so as to overtop the tallest trees, and while the Tyrians from terror could neither fight nor fly, slew some with his fangs, others in his folds, and others with his poisonous breath.

Cadmus having waited for the return of his men until midday, went in search of them. His covering was a lion's hide, and besides his javelin he carried in his hand a lance, and in his breast a bold heart, a surer reliance than either. When he entered the wood and saw the lifeless bodies of his men, and the monster with his bloody jaws, he exclaimed, "O faithful friends, I will avenge you, or share your death." So saying he lifted a huge stone and threw it with all his force at the serpent. Such a block would have shaken the wall of a fortress, but it made no impression on the monster. Cadmus next threw his javelin, which met with better success, for it penetrated the serpent's scales, and pierced through to his entrails. Fierce with pain the monster turned back his head to view the wound, and attempted to draw out the weapon with his mouth, but broke it off, leaving the iron point rankling in his flesh. His neck swelled with rage, bloody foam covered his jaws, and the breath of his nostrils poisoned the air around. Now he twisted himself into a circle, then stretched himself out on the ground like the trunk of a fallen tree. As he moved onward, Cadmus retreated before him, holding his spear opposite to the monster's opened jaws. The serpent snapped at the weapon and attempted to bite its iron point. At last Cadmus, watching his chance, thrust the spear at a moment when the animal's thrown back came against the trunk of a tree, and so succeeded in pinning him to its side. His weight bent the tree as he struggled in the agonies of death. While Cadmus stood over his conquered foe, contemplating its vast size, a voice was heard (whence he knew not, but he heard it distinctly), commanding him to take the dragon's teeth and sow them in the earth. He obeyed. He made a furrow in the ground and planted the teeth, destined to produce a crop of men. Scarce had he done so when the clods began to move, and the points of spears to appear above the sur-

face. Next helmets, with their nodding plumes, came up, and next, the shoulders and breasts and limbs of men with weapons, and in time a harvest of armed warriors. Cadmus, alarmed, prepared to encounter a new enemy, but one of them said to him, "Meddle not with our civil war." With that he who had spoken smote one of his earth-born brothers with a sword, and he himself fell pierced with an arrow from another. The latter fell victim to a fourth, and in like manner the whole crowd dealt with each other until all fell slain with mutual wounds except five survivors. One of these cast away his weapons and said, "Brothers, let

Jacob Jordaens, *Cadmus and Minerva,* 17th century, oil on canvas, Prado, Madrid

us live in peace!" These five joined with Cadmus in building his city, to which they gave the name of Thebes.

Cadmus obtained in marriage Harmonia, the daughter of Venus. The gods left Olympus to honor the occasion with their presence, and Vulcan presented the bride with a necklace of surpassing brilliancy, his own workmanship. But a fatality hung over the family of Cadmus in consequence of his killing the serpent sacred to Mars. Semele and Ino, his daughters, and Actaeon and Pentheius, his grandchildren, all perished unhappily; and Cadmus and Harmonia quitted Thebes, now grown odious to them, and emigrated to the country of the Enchelians, who received them with honor and made Cadmus their king. But the misfortunes of their children still weighed upon their minds; and one day Cadmus exclaimed, "If a serpent's life is so dear to the gods, I would I were myself a serpent." No sooner had he uttered the words than he began to change his form. Harmonia beheld it, and prayed to the gods to let her share his fate. Both became serpents. They lie in the woods, but mindful of their origin they neither avoid the presence of man nor do they ever injure any one.

THE MYRMIDONS

The Myrmidons were the soldiers of Achilles in the Trojan War. From them all zealous and unscrupulous followers of a political chief are called by that name down to this day. But the origin of the Myrmidons would not give one the idea of a fierce and bloody race, but rather of a laborious and peaceful one. Cephalus, king of Athens, arrived in the island of Aegina to seek assistance of his old friend and ally Aeacus, the king, in his wars with Minos, king of Crete. Cephalus was kindly received, and the desired assistance readily promised. "I have people enough," said Aeacus, "to protect myself and spare you such a force as you need." "I rejoice to see it," replied Cephalus, "and my wonder has been raised, I confess, to find such a host of youths as I see around me, all apparently of about the same age. Yet there are many individuals whom I previously knew that I look for now in vain. What has become of them?" Aeacus groaned, and replied with

a voice of sadness, "I have been intending to tell you, and will now do so without more delay, that you may see how from the saddest beginning a happy result sometimes flows. Those whom you formerly knew are now dust and ashes! A plague sent by angry Juno devastated the land. She hated it because it bore the name of one of her husband's female favorites. While the disease appeared to spring from natural causes we resisted it as we best might by natural remedies; but it soon appeared that the pestilence was too powerful for our efforts, and we yielded. At the beginning the sky seemed to settle down upon the earth, and thick clouds shut in the heated air. For four months together a deadly south wind prevailed. The disorder affected the wells and springs; thousands of snakes crept over the land and shed their poison in the fountains. The force of the disease was first spent on the lower animals; dogs, cattle, sheep, and birds. The luckless plowman wondered to see his oxen fall in the midst of their work, and lie helpless in the unfinished furrow. The wool fell from the bleating sheep, and their bodies pined away. The horse, once foremost in the race, contested the palm no more, but groaned at his stall, and died an inglorious death. The wild boar forgot his rage, the stag his swiftness, the bears no longer attacked the herds. Everything languished; dead bodies lay in the roads, the fields, and the woods; the air was poisoned by them. I tell you what is hardly credible, but neither dogs nor birds would touch them, nor starving wolves. Their decay spread the infection. Next the disease attacked the country people, and then the dwellers in the city. At first the cheek was flushed, and the breath drawn with difficulty. The tongue grew rough and swelled, and the dry mouth stood open with its veins enlarged and gasped for the air. Men could not bear the heat of their clothes or their beds, but preferred to lie on the bare ground; and the ground did not cool them, but on the contrary, they heated the spot where they lay. Nor could the physicians help, for the disease attacked them also, and the contact of the sick gave them infection, so that the most faithful were the first victims. At last all hope of relief vanished and men learned to look upon death as the only deliverer from disease. Then they gave way to every inclination, and cared not to ask what was expedient, for nothing was expedient. All restraint laid aside, they crowded around the wells and fountains, and drank until they died, without quenching thirst. Many had not strength to get away from the water but died in the midst of the stream, and others would drink of it notwithstanding. Such was their weariness of their sickbeds that some would creep forth, and if not strong enough to stand, would die on the ground. They seemed to hate their friends, and got away from their homes, as if, not knowing the cause of their sickness, they charged it on the place of their abode. Some were seen tottering along the road, as long as they could stand, while others sank on the earth, and turned their dying eyes around to take a last look, then closed them in death.

"What heart had I left me, during all this, or what ought I to have had, except to hate life and wish to be with my dead subjects? On all sides lay my people strewn like over-ripened apples beneath the tree, or acorns under the storm-shaken oak. You see yonder temple on the height. It is sacred to Jupiter. Oh, how many offered prayers there; husbands for wives, fathers for sons, and died in the very act of supplication! How often, while the priest made ready for sacrifice, the victim fell, struck down by disease without waiting for the blow. At length all reverence for sacred things was lost. Bodies were thrown out unburied, wood was wanting for funeral piles, men fought with one another for the possession of them. Finally there were none left to mourn; sons and husbands, old men and youths, perished alike unlamented."

Standing before the altar I raised my eyes to heaven. 'Oh, Jupiter,' I said, 'if thou art indeed my father, and art not ashamed of thy offspring, give me back my people, or take me also away!' At these words a clap of thunder was heard. 'I accept the omen,' I cried; 'oh, may it be a sign of a favorable disposition towards me!' By chance there grew by the place where I stood an oak with wide-spreading branches, sacred to Jupiter. I observed a troop of ants busy with their labor, carrying minute grains in their mouths and following one another in a line up the trunk of the tree. Observing their numbers with admiration, I said, 'Give me, oh father,

citizens as numerous as these, and replenish my empty city.' The tree shook and gave a rustling sound with its branches though no wind agitated them. I trembled in every limb, yet I kissed the earth and the tree. I would not confess to myself that I hoped, yet I did hope. Night came on and sleep took possession of my frame oppressed with cares. The tree stood before me in my dreams, with its numerous branches all covered with living, moving creatures. It seemed to shake its limbs and throw down over the ground a multitude of those industrious grain-gathering animals, which appeared to gain in size, and grow larger, and by-and-by to stand erect, lay aside their superfluous legs and their black color, and finally to assume the human form. Then I awoke, and my first impulse was to chide the gods who had robbed me of a sweet vision and given me no reality in its place. Being still in the temple my attention was caught by the sound of many voices without; a sound of late unusual to my ears. While I began to think I was yet dreaming, Telamon, my son, throwing open the temple-gates, exclaimed, 'Father, approach, and behold things surpassing even your hopes!' I went forth; I saw a multitude of men, such as I had seen in my dream, and they were passing in procession in the same manner. While I gazed with wonder and delight they approached, and kneeling, hailed me as their king. I paid my vows to Jove, and proceeded to allot the vacant city to the newborn race, and to parcel out the fields among them. I called them Myrmidons from the ant (myrmex), from which they sprang. You have seen these persons; their dispositions resemble those that they had in their former shape. They are a diligent and industrious race, eager to gain, and tenacious of their gains. Among them you may recruit your forces. They will follow you to the war, young in years and bold in heart."

This description of the plague is copied by Ovid from the account which Thucydides, the Greek historian, gives of the plague of Athens. The historian drew from life, and all the poets and writers of fiction since his day, when they have had occasion to describe a similar scene, have borrowed their details from him.

CHAPTER VIII: NISUS AND SCYLLA. ECHO AND NARCISSUS. HERO AND LEANDER.

NISUS AND SCYLLA

Minos, king of Crete, made war upon Megara. Nisus was king of Megara, and Scylla was his daughter. The siege had now lasted six months, and the city still held out, for it was decreed by fate that it should not be taken so long as a certain purple lock, which glittered among the hair of King Nisus, remained on his head. There was a tower on the city walls, which overlooked the plain where Minos and his army were encamped. To this tower Scylla used to repair and look abroad over the tents of the hostile army. The siege had lasted so long that she had learned to distinguish the persons of the leaders. Minos, in particular, excited her admiration. She admired his graceful deportment; if he threw his javelin, skill seemed combined with force in the discharge; if he drew his bow, Apollo himself could not have done it more gracefully. But when he laid aside his helmet, and in his purple robes bestrode his white horse with its gay caparisons, and reined in its foaming mouth, the daughter of Nisus was hardly mistress of herself; she was almost frantic with admiration. She envied the weapon that he grasped, the reins that he held. She felt as if she could, if it were possible, go to him through the hostile ranks; she felt an impulse to cast herself down from the tower into the midst of his camp, or to open the gates to him, or do anything else, so only it might gratify Minos. As she sat in the tower, she talked thus with herself: "I know not whether to rejoice or grieve at this sad war. I grieve that Minos is our enemy; but I rejoice at any cause that brings him to my sight. Perhaps he would be willing to grant us peace, and receive me as a hostage. I would fly down, if I could, and alight in his camp, and tell him that we yield ourselves to his mercy. But, then, to betray my father! No! Rather would I never see Minos again. And yet no doubt it is sometimes the best thing for a city to be conquered when the conqueror is clement and generous. Minos certainly has right on his side. I think we shall be conquered; and if that must be the end of it, why should not love unbar the gates to him, instead of leaving it to be done by war? Better spare delay and slaughter if we can. And, oh, if any one should wound or kill Minos! No one surely would have the heart to do it; yet ignorantly, not knowing him, one might. I will, I will surrender myself to him, with my country as a dowry, and so put an end to the war. But how? The gates are guarded, and my father keeps the keys; he only stands in my way. Oh, that it might please the gods to take him away! But why ask the gods to do it? Another woman, loving as I do, would remove with her own hands whatever stood in the way of her love. And can any other woman dare more than I? I would encounter fire and sword to gain my object; but here there is no need of fire and sword. I only need my father's purple lock. More precious than gold to me, that will give me all I wish."

While she thus reasoned night came on, and soon the whole palace was buried in sleep. She entered her father's bedchamber and cut off the fatal lock; then passed out of the city and entered the enemy's camp. She demanded to be led to the king, and thus addressed him: "I am Scylla, the daughter of Nisus. I surrender to you my country and my father's house. I ask no reward but yourself; for love of you I have done it. See here the purple lock! With this I give you my father and his kingdom." She held out her hand with the fatal spoil. Minos shrunk back and refused to touch it. "The gods destroy thee, infamous woman," he exclaimed; "disgrace of our time! May neither earth nor sea yield thee a resting place! Surely, my Crete, where Jove himself was cradled, shall not be polluted with such a monster!" Thus he said and gave orders that equitable terms should be allowed to the conquered city, and that the fleet should immediately sail from the island. Scylla was frantic. "Ungrateful man," she exclaimed, "is it thus you leave me? Me who have given you victory, who have sacrificed for you parent and country! I am guilty, I confess, and deserve to die, by not by your hand." As the ships left the shore, she leaped into the water, and seizing the rudder of the one that carried Minos, she was borne along an unwelcome companion of their course. A sea eagle soaring aloft, it was her father who had been changed into that form, seeing her, pounced down upon her, and struck her with his beak and claws. In terror she let go the ship and would have fallen into the water, but some pitying deity changed her into a bird. The sea eagle still cherishes the old animosity; and whenever he espies her in his lofty flight, you may see him dart down upon her, with beak and claws, to take vengeance for the ancient crime.

ECHO AND NARCISSUS

Echo was a beautiful nymph, fond of the woods and hills, where she devoted herself to woodland sports. She was a favorite of Diana and attended her in the chase. But Echo had one failing; she was fond of talking, and whether in chat or argument would have the last word. One day Juno was seeking her husband, who, she had reason to fear, was amusing himself among the nymphs. Echo by her talk contrived to detain the goddess until the nymphs made their escape. When Juno discovered it, she passed sentence upon Echo in these words: "You shall forfeit the use of that tongue with which you have cheated me, except for that one purpose you are so fond of: reply. You shall still have the last word, but no power to speak first."

This nymph saw Narcissus, a beautiful youth, as he pursued the chase upon the mountains. She loved him, and followed his footsteps. Oh, how she longed to address him in the softest accents, and win him to converse, but it was not in her power. She waited with impatience for him to speak first and had her answer ready. One day the youth, being separated from his companions, shouted aloud, "Who's here?" Echo replied, "Here." Narcissus looked around, but seeing no one, called out, "Come." Echo answered, "Come." As no one came, Narcissus called again, "Why do you shun me?" Echo asked the same question. "Let us join one another," said the youth. The maid answered with all her heart in the same words and hastened to the spot, ready to throw her arms about his neck. He started back, exclaiming, "Hands off! I would rather die than you should have me." "Have me," said she; but it was all in vain. He left her, and she went to hide her blushes in the recesses of the woods. From that time forth she lived in caves and among mountain cliffs. Her form faded with grief, until at last all her flesh shrank away. Her bones were changed into rocks, and there was nothing left of her but her voice. With that she is still ready to reply to any one who calls her and keeps up her old habit of having the last word.

Narcissus was cruel not in this case alone. He shunned all the rest of the nymphs as he had done poor Echo. One day a maiden, who had in vain endeavored to attract him, uttered a prayer that he might some time or other feel what it was to love and meet no return of affection. The avenging goddess heard and granted the prayer. There was a clear fountain, with water like silver, to which the shepherds never drove their flocks. Nor did the mountain goats resort to it, nor any of the beasts of the forest; neither was it defaced with fallen leaves or branches; but the grass grew fresh around it, and the rocks sheltered it from the sun. Hither came one day the youth fatigued with hunting, heated and thirsty. He stooped down to drink and saw his own image in the water; he thought it was some beautiful water spirit living in the fountain. He stood gazing with

John William Waterhouse, *Echo and Narcissus*, 1903, oil on canvas, Walker Art Gallery

admiration at those bright eyes, those locks curled like the locks of Bacchus or Apollo, the rounded cheeks, the ivory neck, the parted lips, and the glow of health and exercise over all. He fell in love with himself. He brought his lips near to take a kiss; he plunged his arms in to embrace the beloved object. It fled at the touch but returned again after a moment and renewed the fascination. He could not tear himself away; he lost all thought of food or rest, while he hovered over the brink of the fountain gazing upon his own image. He talked with the supposed spirit: "Why, beautiful being, do you shun me? Surely my face is not one to repel you. The nymphs love me, and you yourself look not indifferent upon me. When I stretch forth my arms you do the same; and you smile upon me and answer my beckonings with the like." His tears fell into the water and disturbed the image. As he saw it depart, he exclaimed, "Stay, I entreat you! Let me at least gaze upon you, if I may not touch you."

With this, and much more of the same kind, he cherished the flame that consumed him, so that by degrees he lost his color, his vigor, and the beauty that formerly had so charmed the nymph Echo. She kept near him, however, and when he exclaimed, "Alas! Alas!" she answered him with the same words. He pined away and died; and when his shade passed the Stygian river, it leaned over the boat to catch a look of itself in the waters. The nymphs mourned for him, especially the water nymphs; and when they smote their breasts, Echo smote hers also. They prepared a funeral pile, and would have burned the body, but it was nowhere to be found; but in its place a flower, purple within, and surrounded with white leaves, which bears the name and preserves the memory of Narcissus.

Edward Burne-Jones, *Hero,* oil on canvas, from an exhibition catalog

HERO AND LEANDER

Leander was a youth of Abydos, a town of the Asian side of the strait that separates Asia and Europe. On the opposite shore in the town of Sestos lived the maiden Hero, a priestess of Venus. Leander loved her, and used to swim the strait nightly to enjoy the company of his mistress, guided by a torch that she reared upon the tower, for the purpose. But one night a tempest arose and the sea was rough; his strength failed, and he was drowned. The waves bore his body to the European shore, where Hero became aware of his death, and in her despair cast herself down from the tower into the sea and perished.

The story of Leander's swimming the Hellespont was looked upon as fabulous, and the feat considered impossible, until Lord Byron proved its possibility by performing it himself. In the Bride of Abydos he says, "These limbs that buoyant wave hath borne." The distance in the narrowest part is almost a mile, and there is a constant current setting out from the Sea of Marmora into the Archipelago. Since Byron's time the feat has been achieved by others; but it yet remains a test of strength and skill in the art of swimming sufficient to give a wide and lasting celebrity to any one of our readers who may dare to make the attempt and succeed in accomplishing it.

CHAPTER IX: MINERVA AND ARACHNE. NIOBE. THE STORY OF PERSEUS.

René-Antoine Houasse, *Minerve et Arachne,* c. 1690 Palace of Versailles

MINERVA AND ARACHNE

Minerva, the goddess of wisdom, was the daughter of Jupiter. She, they say, sprang forth from his brain full grown and clad in complete armor. She presided over the useful and ornamental arts, both those of men, such as agriculture and navigation, and those of women: spinning, weaving, and needlework. She was also a warlike divinity; but a lover of defensive war only. She had no sympathy with Mars's savage love of violence and bloodshed. Athens was her chosen seat, her own city, awarded to her as the prize of a contest with Neptune, who also aspired to it. The tale ran that in the reign of Cecrops, the first king of Athens, the two deities contended for the possession of the city. The gods decreed that it should be awarded to that one who produced the gift most useful to mortals. Neptune gave the horse; Minerva produced the olive. The gods gave judgment that the olive was the more useful of the two and awarded the city to the goddess; and it was named after her, Athens, her name in Greek being Athena.

In another contest, a mortal dared to come in competition with Minerva. That mortal was Arachne, a maiden who had attained such skill in the arts of weaving and embroidery that the nymphs themselves would leave their groves and fountains to come and gaze upon her work. It was not only beautiful when it was done, but beautiful also in the doing. To watch her, as she took the wool in its rude state and formed it into rolls, or separated it with her fingers and carded it until it looked as light and soft as a cloud, or twirled the spindle with skillful touch, or wove the web, or, when woven, adorned it with her needle, one would have said that Minerva herself had taught her. But this she denied and could not bear to be thought a pupil even of a goddess. "Let Minerva try her skill with mine," said she; "if beaten, I will pay the penalty." Minerva heard this and was displeased. Assuming the form of an old woman, she went and gave Arachne some friendly advice. "I have had much experience," said she, "and I hope you will not despise my counsel. Challenge your fellow-mortals as you will, but do not compete with a goddess. On the contrary, I advise you to ask her forgiveness for what you have said, and, as she is merciful, perhaps she will pardon you." Arachne stopped her spinning and looked at the old dame with anger in her countenance. "Keep your counsel," said she, "for your daughters or handmaids; for my part, I know what I say, and I stand to it. I am not afraid of the goddess; let her try her skill, if she dare venture." "She comes," said Minerva; and dropping her disguise, stood confessed. The nymphs bent low in homage, and all the bystanders paid reverence. Arachne alone was unterrified. She blushed, indeed; a sudden color dyed her cheek, and then she grew pale. But she stood to her resolve and with a foolish conceit of her own skill rushed on her fate. Minerva forbore no longer, nor interposed any further advice. They proceed to the contest.

Each takes her station and attaches the web to the beam. Then the slender shuttle is passed in and out among the threads. The reed with its fine teeth strikes up the woof into its place and compacts the web. Both work with speed; their skillful hands move rapidly, and the excitement of the contest makes the labor light. Wool of Tyrian dye is contrasted with that of other colors, shaded off into one another so adroitly that the joining deceives the eye. Like the bow, whose long arch tinges the heavens, formed by sunbeams reflected from the shower (this description of the rainbow is literally translated from Ovid), in which, where the colors meet they seem as one, but at a little distance from the point of contact are wholly different. Minerva wrought on her web the scene of her contest with Neptune. Twelve of the heavenly powers are represented, Jupiter, with august gravity, sitting in the midst. Neptune, the ruler of the sea, holds his trident and appears to have just smitten the earth, from which a horse has leaped forth. Minerva depicted herself with helmed head, her Aegis covering her breast. Such was the central circle; and in the four corners were represented incidents illustrating the displeasure of the gods at such presumptuous mortals as had dared to contend with them. These were meant as warnings to her rival to give up the contest before it was too late. Arachne filled her web with subjects designedly chosen to exhibit the failings and errors of the gods. One scene represented Leda caressing the swan, under which form Jupiter had disguised himself; and another, Danae, in the brazen tower in which her father had imprisoned her, but where the god effected his entrance in the form of a shower of gold. Still another depicted Europa deceived by Jupiter under the disguise of a bull. Encouraged by the tameness of the animal, Europa ventured to mount his back, whereupon Jupiter advanced into the sea, and swam with her to Crete. You would have thought it was a real bull so naturally was it wrought, and so natural was the water in which it swam. She seemed to look with longing eyes back upon the shore she was leaving, and to call to her companions for help. She ap-

Abraham Bloemaert, *Apollo and Diana Punishing Niobe by Killing her Children,* 1591, oil on canvas, Statens Museum fur Kunst

peared to shudder with terror at the sight of the heaving waves, and to draw back her feet from the water. Arachne filled her canvas with these and like subjects, wonderfully well done, but strongly marking her presumption and impiety. Minerva could not forbear to admire, yet felt indignant at the insult. She struck the web with her shuttle, and rent it in pieces; she then touched the forehead of Arachne and made her feel her guilt and shame. She could not endure it, and went and hanged herself.

Minerva pitied her as she saw her hanging by a rope. "Live, guilty woman," said she; " and that you may preserve the memory of this lesson, continue to hang, you and your descendants, to all future times." She sprinkled her with

the juices of aconite, and immediately her hair came off, and her nose and ears likewise. Her form shrank up, and her head grew smaller yet; her fingers grew to her side, and served for legs. All the rest of her is body, out of which she spins her thread, often hanging suspended by it, in the same attitude as when Minerva touched her and transformed her into a spider.

NIOBE

The fate of Arachne was noised abroad through all the country and served as a warning to all presumptuous mortals not to compare themselves with the divinities. But one, and she a matron too, failed to learn the lesson of humility. It was Niobe, the queen of Thebes. She had indeed much to be proud of; but it was not her husband's fame, nor her own beauty, nor their great descent, nor the power of their kingdom that elated her. It was her children; and truly the happiest of mothers would Niobe have been, if only she had not claimed to be so. It was on occasion of the annual celebration in honor of Latona and her offspring, Apollo and Diana, when the people of Thebes were assembled, their brows crowned with laurel, bearing frankincense to the altars and paying their vows, that Niobe appeared among the crowd. Her attire was splendid with gold and gems, and her face as beautiful as the face of an angry woman can be. She stood and surveyed the people with haughty looks. "What folly," said she, "is this! To prefer beings whom you never saw to those who stand before your eyes! Why should Latona be honored with worship rather than I? My father was Tantalus, who was received as a guest at the table of the gods; my mother was a goddess. My husband built and rules this city, Thebes; and Phrygia is my paternal inheritance. Wherever I turn my eyes I survey the elements of my power; nor is my form and presence unworthy of a goddess. To all this let me add, I have seven sons and seven daughters, and look for sons-in-law and daughters-in-law of pretensions worthy of my alliance. Have I not cause for pride? Will you prefer to me this Latona, the Titan's daughter, with her two children? I have seven times as many. Fortunate indeed am I, and fortunate I shall remain! Will any one deny this? My abundance is my security. I feel myself too strong for Fortune to subdue. She may take from me much; I shall still have much left. Were I to lose some of my children, I should hardly be left as poor as Latona with her two only. Away with you from these solemnities, put off the laurel from your brows, have done with this worship!"

The people obeyed, and left the sacred services uncompleted. The goddess was indignant. On top of Mount Cynthus where she dwelt, she thus addressed her son and daughter: "My children, I who have been so proud of you both, and have been used to hold myself second to none of the goddesses except Juno alone, begin now to doubt whether I am indeed a goddess. I shall be deprived of my worship altogether unless you protect me." She was proceeding in this

Arnold Böcklin, *Medusa*, 1878

strain, but Apollo interrupted her. "Say no more," said he; "speech only delays punishment." So said Diana also. Darting through the air, veiled in clouds, they alighted on the towers of the city. Spread out before the gates was a broad plain, where the youth of the city pursued their warlike sports. The sons of Niobe were there among the rest, some mounted on spirited horses richly caparisoned, some driving gay chariots. Ismenos, the first-born, as he guided his foaming steeds, struck with an arrow from above, cried out, "Ah, me!" dropped the reins and fell lifeless. Another, hearing the sound of the bow, like a boatman who sees the storm gathering and makes all sail for the port, gave the rein to his horses and attempted to escape. The inevitable arrow overtook him as he fled. Two others, younger boys, just from their tasks, had gone to the playground to have a game of wrestling. As they stood breast to breast, one arrow pierced them both. They uttered a cry together, together cast a parting look around them, and together breathed their last. Alphenor, an elder brother, seeing them fall, hastened to the spot to render them assistance, and fell stricken in the act of brotherly duty. One only was left, Ilioneus. He raised his arms to heaven to try whether prayer might not avail. "Spare me, ye gods!" he cried, addressing all, in his ignorance that all needed not his intercession; and Apollo would have spared him, but the arrow had already left the string, and it was too late. The terror of the people and grief of the attendants soon made Niobe acquainted with what had taken place. She could hardly think it possible; she was indignant that the gods had dared and amazed that they had been able to do it. Her husband, Amphion, overwhelmed with the blow, destroyed himself. Alas! How different was this Niobe from her who had so lately driven away the people from the sacred rites, and held her stately course through the city, the envy of her friends, now the pity even of her foes! She knelt over the lifeless bodies, and kissed, now one, now another of her dead sons. Raising her pallid arms to heaven, "Cruel Latona," said she, "feed full your rage with my anguish! Satiate your hard heart, while I follow to the grave my seven sons. Yet where is your triumph? Bereaved as I am, I am still richer than you, my conqueror." Scarce had she spoken when the bow sounded and struck terror into all hearts except Niobe's alone. She was brave from excess of grief. The sisters stood in garments of mourning over the biers of their dead brothers. One fell, struck by an arrow, and died on the corpse she was bewailing. Another, attempting to console her mother, suddenly ceased to speak, and sank lifeless to the earth. A third tried to escape by flight, a fourth by concealment, another stood trembling, uncertain what course to take. Six were now dead, and only one remained, whom the mother held clasped in her arms, and covered as it were with her whole body. "Spare me one, and that the youngest! Oh, spare me one of so many!" she cried; and while she spoke, that one fell dead. Desolate she sat, among sons, daughters, husband, all dead, and seemed torpid with grief. The breeze moved not her hair, nor color was on her cheek, her eyes glared fixed and immovable, there was no sign of life about her. Her very tongue clave to the roof of her mouth, and her veins ceased to convey the tide of life. Her neck bent not, her arms made no gesture, her foot no step. She was changed to stone, within and without. Yet tears continued to flow; and, borne on a whirlwind to her native mountain, she still remains, a mass of rock, from which a trickling stream flows, the tribute of her never-ending grief.

THE GRAEAE AND GORGONS

The Graeae were three sisters who were gray-haired from their birth, whence their name. The Gorgons were monstrous females with huge teeth like those of swine, brazen claws, and snaky hair. They also were three in number, two of them immortal, but the other, Medusa, mortal. None of these beings make much figure in mythology except Medusa,

the Gorgon, whose story we shall next advert to. We mention them chiefly to introduce an ingenious theory of some modern writers, namely, that the Gorgons and Graeae were only personifications of the terrors of the sea, the former denoting the strong billows of the wide open main, and the latter the white-crested waves that dash against the rocks of the coast. Their names in Greek signify the above epithets.

PERSEUS AND MEDUSA

Acrisius was the king who ruled in Argos. To him had an oracle declared that he should be slain by the child of his daughter Danae. Therefore the cruel king, thinking it better that Danae should have no children than that he should be slain, ordered a tower of brass to be made, and in this tower he confined his daughter away from all men. But who can

Paolo Veronese, *Perseus Rescuing Andromeda*, 1578, oil on canvas, Museum of Fine Arts, Rennes, France

withstand Jupiter? He saw Danae, loved her, and changing his form to a shower of gold, he shone into the apartment of the captive girl. Perseus was the child of Jupiter and Danae. Acrisius, finding that his precautions had come to nought, and yet hardly daring to kill his own daughter and her young child, placed them both in a chest and sent the chest floating on the sea. It floated away and was finally entangled in the net of Dicte, a fisherman in the island of Seriphus. He brought them to his house and treated them kindly, and in the house of Dicte, Perseus grew up. When Perseus was grown up, Polydectes, king of that country, wishing to send Perseus to his death, bade him go in quest of the head of Medusa. Medusa had once been a beautiful maiden, whose hair was her chief glory, but as she dared to vie in beauty with Minerva, the goddess deprived her of her charms and changed her beautiful ringlets into hissing serpents. She became a cruel monster of so frightful an aspect that no living thing could behold her without being turned into stone. All around the cavern where she dwelt might be seen the stony figures of men and beasts which had chanced to catch a glimpse of her and had been petrified with the sight. Minerva and Mercury aided Perseus. From Minerva, Perseus borrowed her shield, and from Mercury the winged shoes and the harpe or crooked sword. After having flown all over the earth Perseus espied in the bright shield the image of Medusa and her two immortal sisters. Flying down carefully he cut at her with his harpe and severed her head. Putting the trophy in his pouch he flew away just as the two immortal sisters were awakened by the hissings of their snaky locks.

PERSEUS AND ATLAS

After the slaughter of Medusa, Perseus, bearing with him the head of the Gorgon, flew far and wide, over land and sea. As night came on, he reached the western limit of the earth, where the sun goes down. Here he would gladly have rested until morning. It was the realm of King Atlas, whose bulk surpassed that of all other men. He was rich in flocks and herds and had no neighbor or rival to dispute his state. But his chief pride was in his gardens, whose fruit was of gold, hanging from golden branches, half hid with golden

leaves. Perseus said to him, "I come as a guest. If you honor illustrious descent, I claim Jupiter for my father; if mighty deeds, I plead the conquest of the Gorgon. I seek rest and food." But Atlas remembered that an ancient prophecy had warned him that a son of Jove should one day rob him of his golden apples. So he answered, "Begone! Or neither your false claims of glory nor of parentage shall protect you;" and he attempted to thrust him out. Perseus, finding the giant too strong for him, said, "Since you value my friendship so little, deign to accept a present;" and turning his face away, he held up the Gorgon's head. Atlas, with all his bulk, was changed into stone. His beard and hair became forests, his arms and shoulders cliffs, his head a summit, and his bones rocks. Each part increased in bulk until he became a mountain, and (such was the pleasure of the gods) heaven with all its stars rests upon his shoulders. And all in vain was Atlas turned to a mountain, for the oracle did not mean Perseus, but the hero Hercules, who should come long afterwards to get the golden apples for his cousin Eurystheus.

Perseus, continuing his flight, arrived at the country of the Aethiopians, of which Cepheus was king. Cassiopeia, his queen, proud of her beauty, had dared to compare herself to the Sea Nymphs, which roused their indignation to such a degree that they sent a prodigious sea monster to ravage the coast. To appease the deities, Cepheus was directed by the oracle to expose his daughter Andromeda to be devoured by the monster. As Perseus looked down from his aerial height he beheld the virgin chained to a rock, waiting the approach of the serpent. She was so pale and motionless that if it had not been for her flowing tears and her hair that moved in the breeze, he would have taken her for a marble statue. He was so startled at the sight that he almost forgot to wave his wings. As he hovered over her he said, "O virgin, undeserving of those chains, but rather of such as bind fond lovers together, tell me, I beseech you, your name and the name of your country, and why you are thus bound." At first she was silent from modesty, and, if she could, would have hid her face with her hands; but when he repeated his questions, for fear she might be thought guilty of some fault which she dared not tell, she disclosed her name and that of her country, and her mother's pride of beauty. Before she had done speaking, a sound was heard off upon the water, and the sea-monster appeared, with his head raised above the surface, cleaving the waves with his broad breast. The virgin shrieked, the father and mother who had now arrived at the scene, wretched both, but the mother more justly so, stood by, not able to afford protection, but only to pour forth lamentations and to embrace the victim. Then spoke Perseus: "There will be time enough for tears; this hour is all we have for rescue. My rank as the son of Jove and my renown as the slayer of the Gorgon might make me acceptable as a suitor; but I will try to win her by services rendered, if the gods will only be propitious. If she be rescued by my valor, I demand that she be my reward." The parents consent (how could they hesitate?) and promise a royal dowry with her.

Luca Giordano, *Perseus Fighting Phineus and His Companions*, c. 1670, oil on canvas, National Gallery, London

And now the monster is within the range of a stone thrown by a skillful slinger, when with a sudden bound the youth soared into the air. As an eagle, when from his lofty flight he sees a serpent basking in the sun, pounces upon him and seizes him by the neck to prevent him from turning his head round and using his fangs, so the youth darts down upon the back of the monster and plunges his sword into its shoulder. Irritated by the wound the monster raises himself into the air, then plunges into the depth; then, like a wild boar surrounded by a pack of barking dogs, turns swiftly from side to side, while the youth eludes its attacks by means of his wings. Wherever he can find a passage for his sword between the scales he makes a wound, piercing now the side, now the flank, as it slopes towards the tail. The brute spouts from his nostrils water mixed with blood. The wings of the hero are wet with it, and he dares no longer trust to them. Alighting on a rock that rose above the waves, and holding on by a projecting fragment, as the monster floats near he gives him a death-stroke.

The people who had gathered on the shore shouted so that the hills re-echoed to the sound. The parents, transported with joy, embraced their future son-in-law, calling him their deliverer and the savior of their house, and the virgin, both cause and reward of the contest, descended from the rock.

Cassiopeia is called "the starred Aethiop queen," because after her death she was placed among the stars, forming the constellation of that name. Though she attained this honor, yet the Sea Nymphs, her old enemies, prevailed so far as to cause her to be placed in that part of the heaven near the pole, where every night she is half the time held with her head downward, to give her a lesson of humility.

THE WEDDING FEAST

The joyful parents, with Perseus and Andromeda, repaired to the palace, where a banquet was spread for them, and all was joy and festivity. But suddenly a noise was heard of warlike clamor, and Phineus, the betrothed of the virgin, with a party of his adherents, burst in, demanding the maiden as his own. It was in vain that Cepheus remonstrated: "You should have claimed her when she lay bound to the rock, the monster's victim. The sentence of the gods dooming her to such a fate dissolved all engagements, as death itself would have done." Phineus made no reply, but hurled his javelin at Perseus, but it missed its mark and fell harmless. Perseus would have thrown his in turn, but the cowardly assailant ran and took shelter behind the altar. But his act was a signal for an onset by his band upon the guests of Cepheus. They defended themselves and a general conflict ensued, the old king retreating from the scene after fruitless expostulations, calling the gods to witness that he was guiltless of this outrage on the rights of hospitality. Perseus and his friends maintained for some time the unequal contest; but the numbers of the assailants were too great for them, and destruction seemed inevitable, when a sudden thought struck Perseus: "I will make my enemy defend me." Then, with a loud voice he exclaimed, "If I have any friend here let him turn away his eyes!" and held aloft the Gorgon's head. "Seek not to frighten us with your jugglery," said Thescelus and raising his javelin became stone in the very attitude. Ampyx was about to plunge his sword into the body of a prostrate foe, but his arm stiffened and he could neither thrust forward nor withdraw it. Another, in the midst of a vociferous challenge, stopped, his mouth open, but no sound issuing. One of Perseus's friends, Aconteus, caught sight of the Gorgon and stiffened like the rest. Astyages struck him with his sword, but instead of wounding, it recoiled with a ringing noise. Phineus beheld this dreadful result of his unjust aggression, and felt confounded. He called aloud to his friends, but got no answer; he touched them and found them stone. Falling on his knees and stretching out his hands to Perseus, but turning his head away, he begged for mercy. "Take all," said he, "give me but my life." "Base coward," said Perseus, "thus much I will grant you; no weapon shall touch you; moreover you shall be preserved in my house as a memorial of these events." So saying, he held the Gorgon's head to the side where Phineus was looking, and in the very form in which he knelt, with his hands outstretched and face averted, he became fixed immovably,

a mass of stone! Then Perseus returned to Seriphus to King Polydectes and to his mother Danae and the fisherman Dicte. He marched up the tyrant's hall, where Polydectes and his guests were feasting. "Have you the head of Medusa?" exclaimed Polydectes. "Here it is," answered Perseus, and showed it to the king and to his guests. The ancient prophecy that Acrisius had so much feared at last came to pass. For, as Perseus was passing through the country of Larissa, he entered into competition with the youths of the country at the game of hurling the discus. King Acrisius was among the spectators. The youths of Larissa threw first, and then Perseus. His discus went far beyond the others, and, seized by a breeze from the sea, fell upon the foot of Acrisius. The old king swooned with pain, and was carried away from the place only to die. Perseus, who had heard the story of his birth and parentage from Danae, when he learned who Acrisius was, filled with remorse and sorrow, went to the oracle at Delphi, and there was purified from the guilt of homicide. Perseus gave the head of Medusa to Minerva, who had aided him so well to obtain it. Minerva took the head of her once beautiful rival and placed it in the middle of her Aegis.

Of Atlas there is another story, which I like better than the one told. He was one of the Titans who warred against Jupiter like Typhoeus, Briareus, and others. After their defeat by the king of gods and men, Atlas was condemned to stand in the far western part of the earth, by the Pillars of Hercules, and to hold on his shoulders the weight of heaven and the stars. The story runs that Perseus, flying by, asked and obtained rest and food. The next morning he asked what he could do to reward Atlas for his kindness. The best that giant could think of was that Perseus should show him the snaky head of Medusa, that he might be turned to stone and be at rest from his heavy load.

CHAPTER X: MONSTERS. GIANTS. SPHINX. PEGASUS AND THE CHIMAERA. CENTAURS.

Monsters, in the language of mythology, were beings of unnatural proportions or parts, usually regarded with terror, as possessing immense strength and ferocity, which they employed for the injury and annoyance of men. Some of them were supposed to combine the members of different animals; such were the Sphinx and the Chimaera; and to these all the terrible qualities of wild beasts were attributed, together with human sagacity and faculties. Others, as the giants, differed from men chiefly in their size; and in this particular we must recognize a wide distinction among them. The human giants, if so they may be called, such as the Cyclopes, Antaeus, Orion, and others, must be supposed not to be altogether disproportioned to human beings, for they mingled in love and strife with them. But the superhuman giants, who warred with the gods, were of vastly larger dimensions. Tityus, we are told, when stretched on the plain, covered nine acres, and Enceladus required the whole of Mount Aetna to be laid upon him to keep him down. We have already spoken of the war that the giants waged against the gods, and of its result. While this war lasted the giants proved a formidable enemy. Some of them, like Briareus, had a hundred arms; others, like Typhon, breathed out fire. At one time they put the gods to such fear that they fled into Egypt and hid themselves under various forms. Jupiter took the form of a ram, whence he was afterwards worshiped in Egypt as the god Ammon, with curved horns. Apollo became a crow, Bacchus a goat, Diana a cat, Juno a cow, Venus a fish, Mercury a bird. At another time the giants attempted to climb up into heaven and for that purpose took up the mountain Ossa and piled it on Pelion. They were at last subdued by thunderbolts, which Minerva invented and taught Vulcan and his Cyclopes to make for Jupiter.

THE SPHINX

An oracle warned Laius, king of Thebes, that there was danger to his throne and life if his newborn son should be suffered to grow up. He therefore committed the child to the care of a herdsman, with orders to destroy him; but the herdsman, moved to pity, yet not daring entirely to disobey, tied up the child by the feet, and left him hanging to the branch of a tree. Here a herdsman of Polybus, king of Corinth, who was pasturing his flock upon Mount Cithaeron, found the infant. Polybus and Merope, his wife, adopted the child, whom they called Oedipus, or Swollenfoot, for they had no children themselves, and in Corinth Oedipus grew up. But as Oedipus was at Delphi, the oracle prophesied to him that he should kill his father and marry his own mother. Fighting against Fate, Oedipus resolved to leave Corinth and his parents, for he thought that the oracle meant Polybus and Merope. Soon afterwards, Laius being on his way to Delphi, accompanied only by one attendant, met in a narrow road a young man also driving in a chariot. On his refusal to leave the way at their command, the attendant killed one of his horses, and the stranger, filled with rage, slew both Laius and his attendant. The young man was Oedipus, who thus unknowingly became the slayer of his own father. Shortly after this event the city of Thebes was afflicted with a monster that infested the high road. It was called the Sphinx. It had the body of a

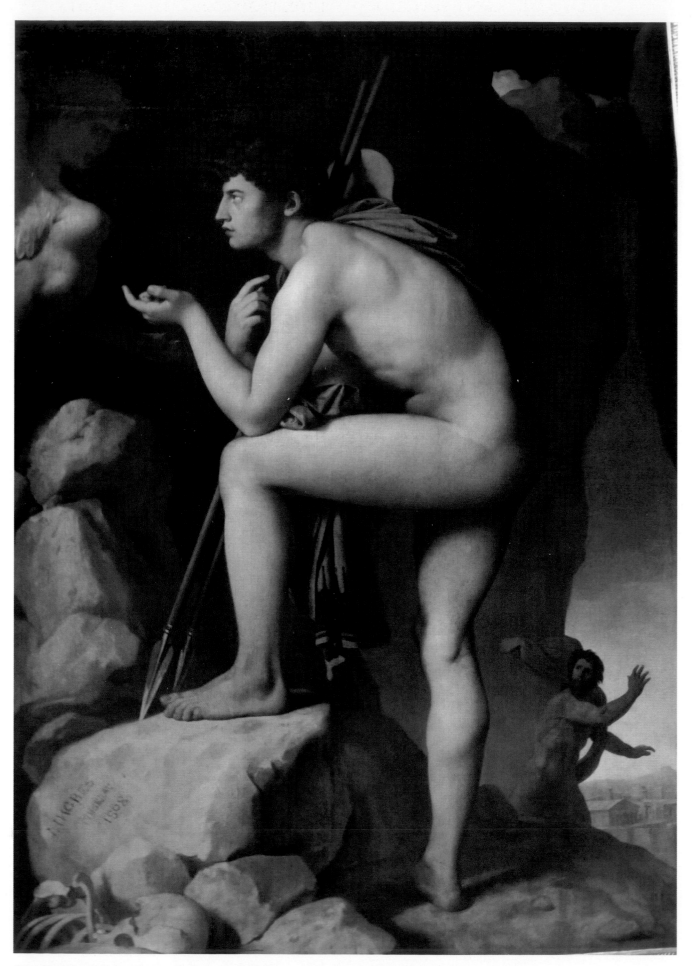

Jean-Auguste-Dominique Ingres, *Oedipus and the Sphinx,* c. 1808, oil on canvas, Louvre, Paris (Photograph © Saliko)

lion, and the upper part of a woman. It lay crouched on the top of a rock, and stopped all travelers who came that way, proposing to them a riddle, with the condition that those who could solve it should pass safe, but those who failed should be killed. Not one had yet succeeded in solving it, and all had been slain. Oedipus was not daunted by these alarming accounts, but boldly advanced to the trial. The Sphinx asked him, "What animal is that which in the morning goes on four feet, at noon on two, and in the evening upon three?" Oedipus replied, "Man, who in childhood creeps on hands and knees, in manhood walks erect, and in old age with the aid of a staff." The Sphinx was so mortified at the solving of her riddle that she cast herself down from the rock and perished. The gratitude of the people for their deliverance was so great that they made Oedipus their king, giving him in marriage their queen Jocasta. Oedipus, ignorant of his parentage, had already become the slayer of his father; in marrying the queen he became the husband of his mother. These horrors remained undiscovered, until at length Thebes was afflicted with famine and pestilence, and the oracle being consulted, the double crime of Oedipus came to light. Jocasta put an end to her own life, and Oedipus, seized with madness, tore out his eyes, and wandered away from Thebes, dreaded and abandoned by all except his daughters, who faithfully adhered to him; until after a tedious period of miserable wandering, he found the termination of his wretched life.

PEGASUS AND THE CHIMAERA

When Perseus cut off Medusa's head, the blood sinking into the earth produced the winged horse Pegasus. Minerva caught and tamed him, and presented him to the Muses. The fountain Hippocrene, on the Muses' mountain Helicon, was opened by a kick from his hoof. The Chimaera was a fearful monster, breathing fire. The fore part of its body was a compound of the lion and the goat, and the hind part a dragon's. It made great havoc in Lycia, so that the king Iobates sought for some hero to destroy it. At that time there arrived at his court a gallant young

Bellerophon Mounted on Pegasus, **Central medallion of Roman mosaic discovered in Autun, France in 1830** (Photograph © Félix Potuit)

warrior, whose name was Bellerophon. He brought letters from Proetus, the son-in-law of Iobates, recommending Bellerophon in the warmest terms as an unconquerable hero, but added at the close a request to his father-in-law to put him to death. The reason was that Proetus was jealous of him, suspecting that his wife Antea looked with too much admiration on the young warrior. From this instance of Bellerophon being unconsciously the bearer of his own death warrant, the expression "Bellerophontic letters" arose, to describe any species of communication that a person is made the bearer of, containing matter prejudicial to himself. Iobates, on perusing the letters, was puzzled what to do, not willing to violate the claims of hospitality, yet wishing to oblige his son-in-law. A lucky thought occurred to him, to send Bellerophon to combat with the Chimaera. Bellerophon accepted the proposal, but before proceeding to the combat consulted the soothsayer Polyidus, who advised him to procure if possible the horse Pegasus for the conflict. For this purpose he directed him to pass the night in the temple of Minerva. He did so, and as he slept Minerva came to him and gave him a golden bridle. When he awoke the bridle remained in his hand. Minerva also showed him Pegasus drinking at the well of Pirene, and at sight of the bridle, the winged steed came willingly and suffered himself to be taken. Bellerophon mounting, rose with him into the air, and soon found the Chimaera, and gained an easy victory over the monster. After the conquest of the Chimaera, Bellerophon was exposed to further trials and labors by his unfriendly host, but by the aid of Pegasus he triumphed in them all; until at length Iobates, seeing that the hero was a special favorite of the gods, gave him his daughter in marriage and made him his successor on the throne. At last Bellerophon by his pride and presumption drew upon himself the anger of the gods; it is said he even attempted to fly up into heaven on his winged steed; but Jupiter sent a gadfly which stung Pegasus and made him throw his rider, who became lame and blind in consequence. After this Bellerophon wandered lonely through the Aleian field, avoiding the paths of men, and died miserably

THE CENTAURS

The Greeks loved to people their woods and hills with strange wild people, half man, half beast. Such were the Satyrs, men with goats' legs. But nobler and better were the Centaurs, men to the waist, while the rest was the form of a horse. The ancients were too fond of the horse to consider the union of his nature with man's as forming any very degraded compound, and accordingly the Centaur is the only one of the fancied monsters of antiquity to which any good traits are assigned. The Centaurs were admitted to the companionship of man, and at the marriage of Pirithous with Hippodamia, they were among the guests. At the feast, Eurytion, one of the Centaurs, becoming intoxicated with the wine, attempted to offer violence to the bride; the other Centaurs followed his example, and a dreadful conflict arose in which several of them were slain. This is the celebrated battle of the Lapithae and Centaurs, a favorite subject with the sculptors and poets of antiquity. But all the Centaurs were not like the rude guests of Pirithous. Chiron was instructed by Apollo and Diana and was renowned for his skill in hunting, medicine, music, and the art of prophecy. The most distinguished heroes of Grecian story were his pupils. Among the rest, the infant Aesculapius was entrusted to his charge, by Apollo, his father. When the sage returned to his home bearing the infant, his daughter Ocyroe came forth to meet him, and at sight of the child burst forth into a prophetic strain (for she was a prophetess), foretelling the glory that he was to achieve. Aesculapius, when grown up, became a renowned physician, and even in one instance succeeded in restoring the dead to life. Pluto resented this, and Jupiter, at his request, struck the bold physician with lightning and killed him, but after his death received him into the number of the gods. Chiron was the wisest and fairest of all the Centaurs, and at his death Jupiter placed him among the stars as the constellation Sagittarius.

CHAPTER XI: THE GOLDEN FLEECE. MEDEA. THE CALYDONIAN HUNT.

THE GOLDEN FLEECE

In very ancient times there lived in Thessaly a king and queen named Athamas and Nephele. They had two children, a boy and a girl. After a time Athamas grew indifferent to his wife, put her away, and took another. Nephele suspected danger to her children from the influence of the stepmother and took measures to send them out of her reach. Mercury assisted her and gave her a ram, with a golden fleece, on which she set the two children, trusting that the ram would convey them to a place of safety. The ram sprung into the air with the children on his back, taking his course to the east, until when crossing the strait that divides Europe and Asia, the girl, whose name was Helle, fell from his back into the sea, which from her was called the Hellespont, now the Dardanelles. The ram continued his career until he reached the kingdom of Colchis, on the eastern shore of the Black Sea, where he safely landed the boy Phyrxus, who was hospitably received by Aeetes, the king of the country. Phryxus sacrificed the ram to Jupiter and gave the Golden Fleece to Aeetes, who placed it in a consecrated grove, under the care of a sleepless dragon. There was another kingdom in Thessaly near to that of Athamas, ruled over by a relative of his. The king Aeson, being tired of the cares of government, surrendered his crown to his brother Pelias, on condition that he should hold it only during the minority of Jason, the son of Aeson. When Jason was grown up and came to demand the crown from his uncle, Pelias pretended to be willing to yield it, but at the same time suggested to the young man the glorious adventure of going in quest of the golden fleece, which it was well known was in the kingdom of Colchis, and was, as Pelias pretended, the rightful property of their family. Jason was pleased with the thought and forthwith made preparations for the expedition.

At that time the only species of navigation known to the Greeks consisted of small boats or canoes hollowed out from trunks of trees, so that when Jason employed Argus to build him a vessel capable of containing fifty men, it was considered a gigantic undertaking. It was accomplished, however, and the vessel was named the Argo, from the name of the builder. Jason sent his invitation to all the adventurous young men of Greece, and soon found himself at the head of a band of bold youths, many of whom afterwards were renowned among the heroes and demigods of Greece. Hercules, Theseus, Orpheus, and Nestor were among them. They are called the Argonauts, from the name of their vessel.

The Argo with her crew of heroes left the shores of Thessaly and having touched at the Island of Lemnos, thence crossed to Mysia and thence to Thrace. Here they found the sage Phineus and from him received instruction as to their future course. It seems the entrance of the Euxine Sea was impeded by two small rocky islands, which floated on the surface, and in their tossings and heavings occasionally came together, crushing and grinding to atoms any object that might be caught between them. They were called the Symplegades, or Clashing Islands. Phineus instructed the Argonauts how to pass this dangerous strait. When they reached the islands they let go a dove, which took her way between the rocks, and passed in safety, only losing some feathers of her tail. Jason and his men seized the favorable moment of the rebound, plied their oars with vigor, and passed safe through, though the islands closed behind them, and actually grazed their stern. They now rowed along the shore until they arrived at the eastern end of the sea, and landed at the kingdom of Colchis. Jason made known his message to the Colchian king, Aeetes, who consented to give up the Golden Fleece if Jason would yoke to the plow two fire-breathing bulls with brazen feet, and sow the teeth of the dragon, which Cadmus had slain, and from which it was well known that a crop of armed men would spring up, who would turn their weapons against their producer. Jason accepted the conditions, and a time was set for making the experiment. Previously, however, he found means to plead his cause to Medea, daughter of the king. He promised her marriage, and as they stood before the altar of Hecate, called the goddess to witness his oath. Medea yielded, and by her aid, for she was a potent sorceress, he was furnished with a charm, by which he could encounter safely the breath of the fire-breathing bulls and the weapons

of the armed men. At the time appointed, the people assembled at the grove of Mars, and the king assumed his royal seat, while the multitude covered the hillsides. The brazen-footed bulls rushed in, breathing fire from their nostrils that burned up the herbage as they passed. The sound was like the roar of a furnace and the smoke like that of water upon quicklime. Jason advanced boldly to meet them. His friends, the chosen heroes of Greece, trembled to behold him. Regardless of the burning breath, he soothed their rage with his voice, patted their necks with fearless hands, and adroitly slipped over them the yoke, and compelled them to drag the plow. The Colchians were amazed; the Greeks shouted for joy. Jason next proceeded to sow the dragon's teeth and plow them in. And soon the crop of armed men sprang up, and, wonderful to relate, no sooner had they reached the surface than they began to brandish their weapons and rush upon Jason. The Greeks trembled for their hero, and even she who had provided him a way of safety and taught him how to use it, Medea herself, grew pale with fear. Jason for a time kept

Phrixus and Helle, **Fresco, Pompeii** (Photograph © Stefano Bolignini)

his assailants at bay with his sword and shield, until finding their numbers overwhelming, he resorted to the charm that Medea had taught him. He seized a stone and threw it in the midst of his foes. They immediately turned their arms against one another, and soon there was not one of the dragon's brood left alive. The Greeks embraced their hero, and Medea, if she dared, would have embraced him too. Then Aeetes promised the next day to give them the fleece, and the Greeks went joyfully down to the Argo with the hero Jason in their midst. But that night Medea came down to Jason and bade him make haste and follow her, for that her father proposed the next morning to attack the Argonauts and to destroy their ship. They went together to the grove of Mars, where the Golden Fleece hung guarded by the dreadful dragon, which glared at the hero and his conductor with his great round eyes that

John William Waterhouse, *Jason and Medea*, 1907, oil on canvas, Private collection

Charles André van Loo, *Miss Clarion in Medea,* 1760, oil on canvas, New Palace, Potsdam, Germany

the expedition at Mysia, for Hylas, a youth beloved by him, who, having gone for water, was laid hold of and kept by the nymphs of the spring, fascinated by his beauty. Hercules went in quest of the lad, and while he was absent the Argo put to sea and left him.

MEDEA AND AESON

Amid the rejoicings for the recovery of the Golden Fleece, Jason felt that one thing was wanting, the presence of Aeson, his father, who was prevented by his age and infirmities from taking part in them. Jason said to Medea, "My wife, I would that your arts, whose power I have seen so mighty for my aid, could do me one further service, and take some years from my life to add them to my father's." Medea replied, "Not at such a cost shall it be done, but if my art avails me, his life shall be lengthened without abridging yours." The next full moon she issued forth alone, while all creatures slept; not a breath stirred the foliage, and all was still. To the stars she addressed her incantations, and to the moon and to Hecate. (Hecate was a mysterious divinity sometimes identified with Diana and sometimes with Proserpine. As Diana represents the moonlight splendor of night, so Hecate represents its darkness and terrors. She was the goddess of sorcery and witchcraft, and was believed to wander by night along the earth, seen only by the dogs whose barking told her approach.) She also invoked Tellus, the goddess of the earth, by whose power plants potent for enchantments are produced, and the gods of the woods and caverns, of mountains and valleys, of lakes and rivers, of winds and vapors. While she spoke the stars shone brighter, and presently a chariot descended through the air, drawn by flying serpents. She ascended it, and, borne aloft, made her way to distant regions, where potent plants grew that she knew how to select for her purpose. Nine nights she employed in her search, and during that time came not within the doors of her palace nor under any roof, and shunned all intercourse with mortals. She next erected two altars, the one to Hecate, the other to Hebe, the goddess of youth, and sacrificed a black sheep, pouring libations of milk and wine. She implored Pluto and his stolen bride that they would not hasten to take the old man's life.

never slept. But Medea was prepared, and began her magic songs and spells, and sprinkled over him a sleeping potion that she had prepared by her art. At the smell he relaxed his rage, stood for a moment motionless, then shut those great round eyes that had never been known to shut before, and turned over on his side, fast asleep. Jason seized the fleece, and with his friends and Medea accompanying, hastened to their vessel, before Aeetes, the king, could arrest their departure, and made the best of their way back to Thessaly, where they arrived safe, and Jason delivered the fleece to Pelias, and dedicated the Argo to Neptune. What became of the fleece afterwards we do not know, but perhaps it was found, after all, like many other golden prizes, not worth the trouble it had cost to procure it. It is said that Hercules left

Then she directed that Aeson should be led forth, and having thrown him into a deep sleep by a charm, had him laid on a bed of herbs, like one dead. Jason and all others were kept away from the place, that no profane eyes might look upon her mysteries. Then, with streaming hair, she thrice moved round the altars, dipped flaming twigs in the blood, and laid them thereon to burn. Meanwhile the caldron with its contents was got ready. In it she put magic herbs, with seeds and flowers of acrid juice, stones from the distant East, and sand from the shore of all-surrounding ocean; hoarfrost, gathered by moonlight, a screech owl's head and wings, and the entrails of a wolf. She added fragments of the shells of tortoises, and the liver of stags — animals tenacious of life — and the head and beak of a crow, which outlives nine generations of men. These, with many other things without a name, she boiled together for her purposed work, stirring them up with a dry olive branch; and behold, the branch when taken out instantly became green, and before long was covered with leaves and a plentiful growth of young olives; and as the liquor boiled and bubbled, and sometimes ran over, the grass, wherever the sprinklings fell, shot forth with a verdure like that of spring. Seeing that all was ready, Medea cut the throat of the old man and let out all his blood, and poured into his mouth and into his wound the juices of her caldron. As soon as he had completely imbibed them, his hair and beard laid by their whiteness and assumed the blackness of youth; his paleness and emaciation were gone; his veins were full of blood, his limbs of vigor and robustness.

Medea used her arts here for a good purpose, but not so in another instance, where she made them the instruments of revenge. Pelias, our readers will recollect, was the usurping uncle of Jason, and had kept him out of his kingdom. Yet he must have had some good qualities, for his daughters loved him, and when they saw what Medea had done for Aeson, they wished her to do the same for their father. Medea pretended to consent and prepared her caldron as before. At her request an old sheep was brought and plunged into the caldron. Very soon a bleating was heard in the kettle, and, when the cover was removed, a lamb jumped forth and ran frisking away into the meadow. The daughters of Pelias saw the experiment with delight and appointed a time for their father to undergo the same operation. But Medea prepared her caldron for him in a very different way. She put in only water and a few simple herbs. In the night she with the sisters entered the bedchamber of the old king, while he and his guards slept soundly under the influence of a spell cast upon them by Medea. The daughters stood by the bedside with their weapons drawn but hesitated to strike, until Medea mocked their irresolution. Then, turning away their faces and giving random blows, they smote him with their weapons. He, starting from his sleep, cried out, "My daughters, what are you doing? Will you kill your father?" Their hearts failed them, and the weapons fell from their hands, but Medea struck him a fatal blow and prevented his saying more. Then they placed him in the caldron, and Medea hastened to depart in her serpent-drawn chariot before they discovered her treachery, for their vengeance would have been terrible.

She escaped, however, but had little enjoyment of the fruits of her crime. Jason, for whom she had done so much, wishing to marry Creusa, princess of Corinth, put away Medea. She, enraged at his ingratitude, called on the gods for vengeance, sent a poisoned robe as a gift to the bride, and then killing her own children, and setting fire to the palace, mounted her serpent-drawn chariot and fled to Athens, where she married King Aegeus, the father of Theseus; and we shall meet her again when we come to the adventures of that hero.

THE CALYDONIAN HUNT. MELEAGER AND ATALANTA

The search for the Golden Fleece was undertaken by Jason, aided by heroes from all Greece, or Hellas as it was then called. It was the first of their common undertakings that made the Greeks feel that they were in truth one nation, though split up into many small kingdoms. Another of their great gatherings was for the Calydonian Hunt, and another, the greatest and most famous of all, for the Trojan

War. The hero of the quest for the Golden Fleece was Jason. With the other heroes of the Greeks, he was present at the Calydonian Hunt. But the chief hero was Meleager, the son of Oeneus, king of Calydon, and Althea, his queen. Althea, when her son was born, beheld the three Fates, who, as they spun their fatal thread, foretold that the life of the child should last no longer than a brand then burning upon the hearth. Althea seized and quenched the brand, and carefully preserved it for years, while Meleager grew to boyhood, youth, and manhood. It chanced, then, that Oeneus, as he offered sacrifices to the gods, omitted to pay due honors to Diana, and she, indignant at the neglect, sent a wild boar of enormous size to lay waste the files of Calydon. Its eyes shone with blood and fire, its bristles stood like threatening spears, and its tusks were like those of Indian elephants. The growing corn was trampled, the vines and olive trees

laid waste, the flocks and herds were driven in wild confusion by the slaughtering foe. All common aid seemed vain; but Meleager called on the heroes of Greece to join in a bold hunt for the ravenous monster. Theseus and his friend Pirithous, Jason, Peleus afterwards the father of Achilles, Telamon the father of Ajax, Nestor, then a youth, but who in his age bore arms with Achilles and Ajax in the Trojan war, these and many more joined in the enterprise. With them came Atalanta, the daughter of Iasius, king of Arcadia. A buckle of polished gold confined her vest, an ivory quiver hung on her left shoulder, and her left hand bore the bow. Her face conjoined feminine beauty with the best graces of martial youth. Meleager saw and loved her. But now already they were near the monster's lair. They stretched strong nets from tree to tree; they uncoupled their dogs, they tried to find the footprints of their quarry in the grass.

Jacob Jordaens, *Meleager and Atalanta,* c. 1620, oil on canvas, Prado, Madrid

From the wood is a descent to marshy ground. Here the boar, as he lies among the reeds, heard the shouts of his pursuers, and rushed forth against them. One and another is thrown down and slain. Jason throws his spear with a prayer to Diana for success; and the favoring goddess allows the weapon to touch, but not to wound, removing the steel point of the spear even in its flight. Nestor, assailed, seeks and finds safety in the branches of a tree. Telamon rushes on, but stumbling at a projecting root, falls prone. But an arrow from Atalanta for the first time tastes the monster's blood. It is a slight wound, but Meleager sees and joyfully proclaims it. Anceus, excited to envy by the praise given to a female, loudly proclaims his own valor and defies alike the boar and the goddess who had sent it; but as he rushes on, the infuriated beast lays him low with a mortal wound. Theseus throws his lance, but it is turned aside by a projecting bough. The dart of Jason misses its object and kills instead one of their own dogs. But Meleager, after one unsuccessful stroke, drives his spear into the monsters side, then rushes on and dispatches him with repeated blows.

Then rises a shout from those around; they congratulate the conqueror, crowding to touch his hand. He, placing his foot upon the slain boar, turns to Atalanta and bestows on her the head and the rough hide, the trophies of his success. But at this, envy excites the rest to strife. Phlexippus and Toxeus, the uncles of Meleager and Althea's brothers, beyond the rest oppose the gift, and snatch from the maiden the trophy she has received. Meleager, kindling with rage at the wrong done to himself, and still more at the insult offered to her whom he loves, forgets the claims of kindred and plunges his sword into the offenders' hearts. Althea bearing gifts of thankfulness to the temples for the victory of her son, sees the bodies of her murdered brothers met her sight. She shrieks, and beats her breast, and hastens to change the garments of rejoicing for those of mourning. But when the author of the deed is known, grief gives way to the stern desire of vengeance on her son. The fatal brand, which once she rescued from the flames, the brand which the Fates had linked with Meleager's life, she brings forth, and commands a fire to be prepared.

Then four times she essays to place the brand upon the pile; four times draws back, shuddering at the thought of bringing destruction on her son. The feelings of the mother and the sister contend within her. Now she is pale at the thought of the purposed deed, now flushed again with anger at the act of her son. As a vessel, driven in one direction by the wind, and in the opposite by the tide, the mind of Althea hangs suspended in uncertainty. But now the sister prevails above the mother, and she begins as she holds the fatal wood: "Turn, ye Furies, goddesses of punishment! Turn to behold the sacrifice I bring! Crime must atone for crime. Shall Oeneus rejoice in his victor son, while the house of Thestius (Thestius was father of Toxeus, Phlexippus and Althea) is desolate? But, alas! To what deed am I borne along? Brothers, forgive a mother's weakness! My hand fails me. He deserves death, but not that I should destroy him. But shall he then live, and triumph, and reign over Calydon, while you, my brothers, wander unavenged among the shades? No! Thou hast lived by my gift; die, now, for thine own crime. Return the life that twice I gave thee, first at thy birth, again when I snatched this brand from the flames. O that thou hadst then died! Alas! Evil is the conquest; but, brothers, ye have conquered."

And, turning away her face, she throws the fatal wood upon the burning pile. It seems to give a deadly groan. Meleager, absent and unknowing of the cause, feels a sudden pang. He burns and only by courageous pride conquers the pain that destroys him. He mourns only that he perishes by a bloodless and unhonored death. With his last breath he calls upon his aged father, his brother, and his fond sisters, upon his beloved Atalanta, and upon his mother, the unknown cause of his fate. The flames increase, and with them the pain of the hero. Now both subside; now both are quenched. The brand is ashes and the life of Meleager is breathed forth to the wandering winds.

Althea, when the deed was done, laid violent hands upon herself. The sisters of Meleager mourned their brother with uncontrollable grief; until Diana, pitying the sorrows of the house that once had aroused her anger, turned them into birds.

ATALANTA

The innocent cause of so much sorrow was a maiden whose face you might truly say was boyish for a girl, yet too girlish for a boy. Her fortune had been told, and it was to this effect: "Atalanta, do not marry; marriage will be your ruin." Terrified by this oracle, she fled the society of men, and devoted herself to the sports of the chase. To all suitors (for she had many) she imposed a condition that was generally effectual in relieving her of their persecutions: "I will be the prize of him who shall conquer me in the race; but death must be the penalty of all who try and fail." In spite of this hard condition some would try. Hippomenes was to be judge of the race. "Can it be possible that any will be so rash as to risk so much for a wife?" said he. But when he saw her lay aside her robe for the race, he changed his mind, and said, "Pardon me, youths, I knew not the prize you were competing for." As he surveyed them he wished them all to be beaten and swelled with envy of any one that seemed at all likely to win. While such were his thoughts, the virgin darted forward. As she ran, she looked more beautiful than ever. The breezes seemed to give wings to her feet; her hair flew over her shoulders, and the gay fringe of her garment fluttered behind her. A ruddy hue tinged the whiteness of her skin, such as a crimson curtain casts on a marble wall. All her competitors were distanced, and were put to death without mercy. Hippomenes, not daunted by this result, fixing his eyes on the virgin, said, "Why boast of beating those laggards? I offer myself for the contest." Atalanta looked at him with a pitying countenance, and hardly knew whether she would rather conquer him or not. "What god can tempt one so young and handsome to throw himself away? I pity him, not for his beauty (yet he is beautiful), but for his youth. I wish he would give up the race, or if he will be so mad, I hope he may outrun me." While she hesitates, revolving these thoughts, the spectators grow impatient for the race, and her father prompts her to prepare. Then Hippomenes addressed a prayer to Venus; "Help me, Venus, for you have led me on." Venus heard, and was propitious. In the garden of her temple, in her own island of Cyprus, is a tree with yellow leaves and yellow branches, and golden fruit. Hence Venus gathered three golden apples, and, unseen by all else, gave them to Hippomenes, and told him how to use them.

The signal is given; each starts from the goal and skims over the sand. So light their tread, you would almost have thought they might run over the river surface or over the waving grain without sinking. The cries of the spectators cheered on Hippomenes: "Now, now do your best! Haste, haste! You gain on her! Relax not! One more effort!" It was doubtful whether the youth or the maiden heard these cries with the greater pleasure. But his breath began to fail him, his throat was dry, the goal yet far off. At that moment he threw down one of the golden apples. The virgin was all amazement. She stopped to pick it up. Hippomenes shot ahead. Shouts burst forth from all sides. She redoubled her efforts, and soon overtook him. Again he threw an apple. She stopped again, but again came up with him. The goal was near; one chance only remained. "Now, goddess," said he, "prosper your gift!" and threw the last apple off at one side. She looked at it, and hesitated; Venus impelled her to turn aside for it. She did so and was vanquished. The youth carried off his prize. But the lovers were so full of their own happiness that they forgot to pay due honor to Venus; and the goddess was provoked at their ingratitude. She caused them to give offence to Cybele. That powerful goddess was not to be insulted with impunity. She took from them their human form and turned them into animals of characters resembling their own: of the huntress-heroine, triumphing in the blood of her lovers, she made a lioness, and of her lord and master a lion, and yoked them to her car, there they are still to be seen in all representations, in statuary or painting, of the goddess Cybele.

Cybele is the Latin name of the goddess called by the Greeks Rhea and Ops. She was the wife of Cronos and mother of Zeus. In works of art, she exhibits the matronly air that distinguishes Juno and Ceres. Sometimes she is veiled, and seated on a throne with lions at her side, at other times riding in a chariot drawn by lions. She sometimes wears a mural crown, that is, a crown whose rim is carved in the form of towers and battlements. Her priests were called Corybantes.

Nicolas Colombel, *Hippomenes and Atalanta,* c. 1680, oil on canvas, Liechtenstein Museum

CHAPTER XII: THE LABORS OF HERCULES.

Hercules (in Greek, Heracles) was the son of Jupiter and Alcmena. As Juno was always hostile to the offspring of her husband by mortal mothers, she declared war against Hercules from his birth. She sent two serpents to destroy him as he lay in his cradle, but the precocious infant strangled them with his own hands. He was, however, by the arts of Juno rendered subject to his cousin Eurystheus and compelled to perform all his commands. Eurystheus enjoined upon him a succession of desperate adventures, known as the twelve "Labors of Hercules." The first was the fight with the Nemean lion. The valley of Nemea was infested by a terrible lion; Eurystheus ordered Hercules to bring him the skin of this monster. After using in vain his club and arrows against the lion, Hercules strangled the animal with his hands. He returned carrying the dead lion on his shoulders; but Eurystheus was so frightened at the sight of it and at this proof of the prodigious strength of the hero, that he ordered him to deliver the account of his exploits in future outside the town. His next labor was to slaughter the Hydra. This monster ravaged the country of Argos and dwelt in a swamp near the well of Amymone. The story goes that when the country was suffering from drought, Neptune, who loved her, had permitted her to touch the rock with his trident, and a spring of three outlets burst forth. Here the Hydra took up his position, and Hercules was sent to destroy him. The Hydra had nine heads, of which the middle one was immortal. Hercules struck off its head with his club, but in the place of the head knocked off, two new ones grew forth each time. At length with the assistance of his faithful servant Iolaus, he burned away the heads of the Hydra and buried the ninth or immortal one under a huge rock.

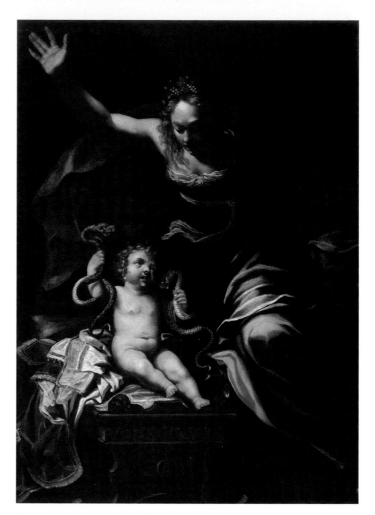

Scene from the Infancy of Hercules, attributed to Bernardo Mei, c. 1676, oil on canvas

Another labor was the cleaning of the Augean stables. Augeas, king of Elis, had a herd of three thousand oxen, whose stalls had not been cleansed for thirty years. Hercules brought the rivers Alpheus and Peneus through them and cleansed them thoroughly in one day. His next labor was of a more delicate kind. Admeta, the daughter of Eurystheus, longed to obtain

84

the girdle of the queen of the Amazons, and Eurystheus ordered Hercules to go and get it. The Amazons were a nation of warlike women and held several flourishing cities. It was their custom to bring up only the female children; the boys were either sent away to the neighboring nations or put to death. Hercules was accompanied by a number of volunteers and after various adventures at last reached the country of the Amazons. Hippolyta, the queen, received him kindly and consented to yield him her girdle; but Juno, taking the form of an Amazon, went among the other Amazons and persuaded them that the strangers were carrying off their queen. The Amazons instantly armed and came in great numbers down to the ship. Hercules, thinking that Hippolyta had acted treacherously, slew her, and taking her girdle, made sail homewards.

Another task enjoined him was to bring to Eurystheus the oxen of Geryon, a monster with three bodies who dwelt in the island Erytheia (the red), so called because it lay at the west, under the rays of the setting sun. This description is thought to apply to Spain, of which Geryon was said to be king. After traversing various countries, Hercules reached at length the frontiers of Libya and Europe, where he raised the two mountains of Calpe and Abyla, as monuments of his progress, or according to another account rent one mountain into two and left half on each side, forming the Straits of Gibraltar, the two mountains being called the Pillars of Hercules. The giant Eurytion and his two-headed dog guarded the oxen, but Hercules killed the giant and his dog and brought away the oxen.

When Hercules was driving home the oxen of Geryon, he encountered the huge giant Cacus, who inhabited a cave on Mount Aventine (one of the seven hills of Rome), and plundered the surrounding country. Cacus stole part of the cattle, while the hero slept. That their foot-prints might not serve to show where they had been driven, he dragged them backward by their tails to his cave; so their tracks all seemed to show that they had gone in the opposite direction. Hercules was deceived by this stratagem,

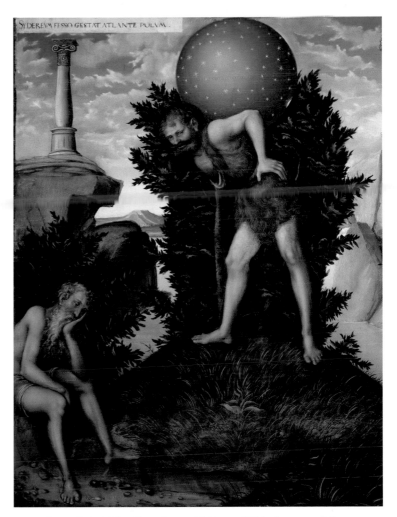

Lucas Cranach the Elder, *Hercules and Atlas,* c. 1537, oil on panel, Herzog Anton Ulrich Museum, Braunschweig, Germany

and would have failed to find his oxen, if it had not happened that in driving the remainder of the herd past the cave where the stolen ones were concealed, those within began to low and were thus discovered. Cacus was slain by Hercules, and Hercules was able to bring the oxen safely back to Eurystheus.

The most difficult labor of all was bringing him the golden apples of the Hesperides, for Hercules did not know where to find them. These were the apples that Juno had received at her wedding from the goddess of the Earth, and which she had entrusted to the keeping of the daughters of Hesperis, assisted by a watchful dragon. After various adventures Hercules arrived at Mount Atlas in Africa. Atlas was one of the Titans who had warred against the gods, and after they were subdued, Atlas was condemned to bear on his shoulders the weight of the heavens. He was the father of the Hesperides, and Hercules thought he might, if any one could, find the apples and bring them to him. But how to send Atlas away from his post of bearing up the heavens?

Hercules took the burden on his own shoulders and sent Atlas to seek the apples. He returned with them, and though somewhat reluctantly, took his burden upon his shoulders again, letting Hercules return with the apples to Eurystheus. The poets, led by the analogy of the lovely appearance of the western sky at sunset, viewed the west as a region of

Frederick Leighton, *The Garden of Hesperides*, c. 1892, oil on canvas, Lady Lever Art Gallery

brightness and glory. Hence they placed in it the Isles of the Blest, the ruddy isle Erytheia, on which the bright oxen of Geryon were pastured, and the isle of the Hesperides. The apples are supposed by some to be the oranges of Spain, of which the Greeks had heard some obscure accounts.

Another celebrated exploit of Hercules was his victory over Antaeus. Antaeus, the son of Terra (the Earth) was a mighty giant and wrestler, whose strength was invincible so long as he remained in contact with his mother Earth. He compelled all strangers who came to his country to wrestle with him, on condition that if conquered (as they all were), they should be put to death. Hercules encountered him, and finding that it was of no avail to throw him, for he always rose with renewed strength from every fall, he lifted him up from the earth and strangled him in the air.

The last exploit we shall record was bringing Cerberus from the lower world. Hercules descended into Hades, accompanied by Mercury and Minerva. He obtained permission from Pluto to carry Cerberus to the upper air, provided he could do it without the use of weapons; and in spite of the monster's struggling he seized him, held him fast, and carried him to Eurystheus, and afterwards brought him back again. When he was in Hades he obtained the liberty of Theseus, his admirer and imitator, who had been detained a prisoner there for an unsuccessful attempt to carry off Proserpine.

Hercules in a fit of madness killed his friend Iphitus and was condemned for this offence to become the slave of Queen Omphale for three years. While in this service the hero's nature seemed changed. He lived effeminately, wearing at times the dress of a woman, and spinning wool with the handmaidens of Omphale, while the queen wore his lion's skin. When this service was ended he married Dejanira and lived in peace with her three years. On one occasion as he was travelling with his wife, they came to a river, across which the Centaur Nessus carried travelers for a stated fee. Hercules himself forded the river but gave Dejanira to Nessus to be carried across. Nessus attempted to run away with

Hans Sebald Beham, *Hercules Capturing Cerberus,* 1545, engraving, Los Angeles County Museum of Art

her, but Hercules heard her cries, and shot an arrow into the heart of Nessus. The dying Centaur told Dejanira to take a portion of his blood and keep it, as it might be used as a charm to preserve the love of her husband. Dejanira did so, and before long fancied she had occasion to use it. Hercules in one of his conquests had taken prisoner a fair maiden, named Iole, of whom he seemed fonder than Dejanira liked. When Hercules was about to offer sacrifices to the gods in honor of his victory, he sent to his wife for a white robe to use on the occasion. Dejanira, thinking it a good opportunity to try her love spell, steeped the garment in the blood of Nessus. We are to suppose she took care to wash out all traces of it, but the magic power remained, and as soon as the garment became warm on the body of Hercules, the poison penetrated into all his limbs and caused him the most intense agony. In his frenzy he seized Lichas, who had brought him the fatal robe and hurled him into the sea. He wrenched off the garment, but it stuck to his flesh, and with it he tore away whole pieces of his body. In this state he embarked on board a ship and was conveyed home. Dejanira on seeing what she had unwittingly done, hung herself. Hercules, prepared to die, ascended Mount Oeta, where he built a funeral pile of trees, gave his bow and arrows to Philoctetes, and laid himself down on the pile,

Bartolomeus Spranger, *Hercules, Dejanira and the Centaur Nessus,* c. 1580, oil on canvas, Kunsthistorisches Museum, Vienna

The gods themselves felt troubled at seeing the champion of the earth so brought to his end; but Jupiter with cheerful countenance thus addressed them: "I am pleased to see your concern, my princes, and am gratified to perceive that I am the ruler of a loyal people, and that my son enjoys your favor. For although your interest in him arises from his noble deeds, yet it is not the less gratifying to me. But now I say to you, Fear not. He who conquered all else is not to be conquered by those flames that you see blazing on Mount Oeta. Only his mother's share in him can perish; what he derived from me is immortal. I shall take him, dead to earth, to the heavenly shores, and I require of you all to receive him kindly. If any of you feel grieved at his attaining this honor, yet no one can deny that he has deserved it." The gods all gave their assent; Juno only heard the closing words with some displeasure that she should be so particularly pointed at, yet not enough to make her regret the determination of her husband. So when the flames had consumed the mother's share of Hercules, the diviner part, instead of being injured thereby, seemed to start forth with new vigor, to assume a more lofty port and a more awful dignity. Jupiter enveloped him in a cloud and took him up in a four-horse chariot to dwell among the stars. As he took his place in heaven, Atlas felt the added weight. Juno, now reconciled to him, gave him her daughter Hebe in marriage.

HEBE AND GANYMEDE

Hebe, the daughter of Juno, and goddess of youth, was cupbearer to the gods. The usual story is, that she resigned her office on becoming the wife of Hercules. According to this, Hebe was dismissed from her office in consequence of a fall which she met with one day when in attendance on the gods. Her successor was Ganymede, a Trojan boy whom Jupiter, in the disguise of an eagle, seized and carried off from the midst of his playfellows on Mount Ida, bore up to heaven, and installed in the vacant place.

his head resting on his club, and his lion's skin spread over him. With a countenance as serene as if he were taking his place at a festal board, he commanded Philoctetes to apply the torch. The flames spread apace and soon invested the whole mass.

CHAPTER XIII: THESEUS. DAEDALUS. CASTOR AND POLLUX.

THESEUS

Theseus was the son of Aegeus, king of Athens, and of Aethra, daughter of the king of Troezene. He was brought up at Troezene, and, when arrived at manhood, was to proceed to Athens and present himself to his father. Aegeus, on parting from Aethra, before the birth of his son, had placed his sword and shoes under a large stone, and directed her to send his son to him when he became strong enough to roll away the stone and take them from under it. When she thought the time had come, his mother led Theseus to the stone. He removed it with ease and took the sword and shoes. As the roads were infested with robbers, his grandfather pressed him earnestly to take the shorter and safer way to his father's country, by sea; but the youth, feeling in himself the spirit and the soul of a hero, and eager to signalize himself like Hercules, with whose fame all Greece then rang, by destroying the evildoers and monsters that oppressed the country, determined on the more perilous and adventurous journey by land. His first day's journey brought him to Epid-aurus, where dwelt a man named Periphetes, a son of Vulcan. This ferocious savage always went armed with a club of iron, and all travelers stood in terror of his violence. When he saw Theseus approach, he assailed him, but speedily fell beneath the blows of the young hero, who took possession of his club, and bore it ever afterwards as a memorial of his first victory. Several similar contests with the petty tyrants and marauders of the country followed, in all of which Theseus was victorious. One of these evildoers was called Procrustes,

Nicolas Poussin, *Theseus Discovering His Father's Sword*, c. 1638, oil on canvas, Musée Condé, Chantilly, France

89

or the Stretcher. He had an iron bedstead, on which he used to tie all travelers who fell into his hands. If they were shorter than the bed, he stretched their limbs to make them fit it; if they were longer than the bed, he lopped off a portion. Theseus served him as he had served others. Having overcome all the perils of the road, Theseus at length reached Athens, where new dangers awaited him. Medea, the sorceress, who had fled from Corinth after her separation from Jason, had become the wife of Aegeus, the father of Theseus. Knowing by her arts who he was, and fearing the loss of her influence with her husband, if Theseus should be acknowledged as his son, she filled the mind of Aegeus with suspicions of the young stranger and induced him to present him a cup of poison; but at the moment when Theseus stepped forward to take it, the sight of the sword that he wore discovered to his father who he was and prevented the fatal draught. Medea, detected in her arts, fled once more from deserved punishment and arrived in Asia, where the country afterwards called Media received its name from her. Theseus was acknowledged by his father and declared his successor. The Athenians were at that time in deep affliction, on account of the tribute that they were forced to pay to Minos, king of Crete. This tribute consisted of seven youths and seven maidens, who were sent every year to be devoured by the Minotaur, a monster with a bull's body and a human head. It was exceedingly strong and fierce. It was kept in a labyrinth constructed by Daedalus, so artfully contrived that whoever was enclosed in it could by no means find his way out unassisted. Here the Minotaur roamed and was fed with human victims. Theseus resolved to deliver his countrymen from this calamity, or to die in the attempt. Accordingly, when the time of sending off the tribute came, and the youths and maidens were, according to custom, drawn by lot to be sent, he offered himself as one of the victims, in spite of the entreaties of his father. The ship departed under black sails, as usual, which Theseus promised his father to change for white, in case of his returning victorious. When they arrived in Crete, the youths and maidens were exhibited before Minos; and Ariadne, the daughter of the king, being present, became deeply enamored of Theseus, by whom her love

was readily returned. She furnished him with a sword, with which to encounter the Minotaur, and with a clew of thread by which he might find his way out of the labyrinth. He was successful, slew the Minotaur, escaped from the labyrinth, and taking Ariadne as the companion of his way, with his rescued companions sailed for Athens. On their way they stopped at the island of Naxos, where Theseus abandoned Ariadne, leaving her asleep. For Minerva had appeared to Theseus in a dream and warned him that Ariadne was destined to be the wife of Bacchus, the wine-god. On approaching the coast of Attica, Theseus, intent on Ariadne, forgot the signal appointed by his father, and neglected to raise the white sails, and the old king, thinking his son had perished, put an end to his own life. Theseus thus became king of Athens.

One of the most celebrated of the adventures of Theseus is his expedition against the Amazons. He assailed them

Giovanni Battista Cima da Conegliano, *Theseus Killing the Minotaur,* **1505, oil on panel, Museo Poldi Pezzoli, Milan, Italy**

before they had recovered from the attack of Hercules, and carried off their queen, Antiope. The Amazons in their turn invaded the country of Athens and penetrated into the city itself; and the final battle in which Theseus overcame them was fought in the very midst of the city. This battle was one of the favorite subjects of the ancient sculptors and is commemorated in several works of art that are still extant.

The friendship between Theseus and Pirithous was of a most intimate nature, yet it originated in the midst of arms. Pirithous had made an irruption into the plain of Marathon, and carried off the herds of the king of Athens. Theseus went to repel the plunderers. The moment Pirithous beheld him, he was seized with admiration; he stretched out his hand as a token of peace, and cried, "Be judge thyself, what satisfaction dost thou require?" "Thy friendship," replied the Athenian, and they swore inviolable fidelity. Their deeds corresponded to their professions, and they ever continued true brothers in arms. Each of them aspired to espouse a daughter of Jupiter. Theseus fixed his choice on Helen, then but a child, afterwards so celebrated as the cause of the Trojan War, and with the aid of his friend he carried her off. Pirithous aspired to the wife of the monarch of Erebus; and Theseus, though aware of the danger, accompanied the ambitious lover in his descent to the underworld. But Pluto seized and set them on an enchanted rock at his palace gate, where they remained until Hercules arrived and liberated Theseus, leaving Pirithous to his fate.

After the death of Antiope, Theseus married Phaedra, daughter of Minos, king of Crete. Phaedra saw in Hippolytus, the son of Theseus, a youth endowed with all the graces and virtues of his father, and of an age corresponding to her own. She loved him, but he repulsed her advances, and her love was changed to hate. She used her influence over her infatuated husband to cause him to be jealous of his son, and he imprecated the vengeance of Neptune upon him. As Hippolytus was one day driving his chariot along the shore, a sea-monster raised himself above the waters and frightened the horses so that they ran away and dashed the chari-

ot to pieces. Hippolytus was killed, but by Diana's assistance Aesculapius restored him to life. Diana removed Hippolytus from the power of his deluded father and false stepmother and placed him in Italy under the protection of the nymph Egeria. Theseus at length lost the favor of his people and retired to the court of Lycomedes, king of Scyros, who at first received him kindly, but afterwards treacherously slew him. In a later age the Athenian general Cimon discovered the place where his remains were laid and caused them to be removed to Athens, where they were deposited in a temple called the Theseum, erected in honor of the hero.

Theseus is a semi-historical personage. It is recorded of him that he united the several tribes by whom the territory of Attica was then possessed into one state, of which Athens was the capital. In commemoration of this important event, he instituted the festival of Panathenaea, in honor of Minerva, the patron deity of Athens. This festival differed from the other Grecian games chiefly in two particulars. It was peculiar to the Athenians, and its chief feature was a solemn procession in which the Peplus or sacred robe of Minerva was carried to the Parthenon and suspended before the statue of the goddess. The Peplus was covered with embroidery, worked by select virgins of the noblest families in Athens. The procession consisted of persons of all ages and both sexes. The old men carried olive branches in their hands, and the young men bore arms. The young women carried baskets on their heads, containing the sacred utensils, cakes, and all things necessary for the sacrifices. The procession formed the subject of the bas-reliefs by Phidias that embellished the outside of the temple of the Parthenon. A considerable portion of these sculptures is now in the British museum among those known as the "Elgin marbles."

OLYMPIC AND OTHER GAMES

We may mention here the other celebrated national games of the Greeks. The first and most distinguished were the Olympic, founded, it was said, by Jupiter himself. They were celebrated at Olympia in Elis. Vast numbers of spectators flocked to them from every part of Greece, and from

Asia, Africa, and Sicily. They were repeated every fifth year in midsummer and continued five days. They gave rise to the custom of reckoning time and dating events by Olympiads. The first Olympiad is generally considered as corresponding with the year 776 BCE. The Pythian games were celebrated in the vicinity of Delphi, the Isthmian on the Corinthian isthmus, the Nemean at Nemea, a city of Argolis. The exercises in these games were of five sorts: running, leaping, wrestling, throwing the quoit, and hurling the javelin, or boxing. Besides these exercises of bodily strength and agility, there were contests in music, poetry, and eloquence. Thus these games furnished poets, musicians, and authors the best opportunities to present their productions to the public, and the fame of the victors was diffused far and wide.

DAEDALUS

Daedalus, a most skillful artificer, built the labyrinth, from which Theseus escaped by means of the thread of Ariadne. It was an edifice with numberless winding passages and turnings opening into one another, seeming to have neither beginning nor end, like the river Maender, which returns on itself, and flows now onward, now backward, in its course to the sea. Daedalus built the labyrinth for King Minos, but afterwards lost the favor of the king and was shut up in a tower. He contrived to make his escape from his prison but could not leave the island by sea, as the king kept strict watch on all the vessels and permitted none to sail without being carefully searched. "Minos may control the land and sea," said Daedalus, "but not the regions of the air. I will try that way." So he set to work to fabricate wings for himself and his young son Icarus. He wrought feathers together beginning with the smallest and adding larger, so as to form an increasing surface. The larger ones he secured with thread and the smaller with wax, and gave the whole a gentle curvature like the wings of a bird. Icarus, the boy, stood and looked on, sometimes running to gather up the feathers which the wind had blown away, and then handling the wax and working it over with his fingers, by his play impeding his father in his labors.

When at last the work was done, the artist, waving his wings, found himself buoyed upward and hung suspended, poising himself on the beaten air. He next equipped his son in the same manner, and taught him how to fly, as a bird tempts her young ones from the lofty nest into the air. When all was prepared for flight, he said, "Icarus, my son, I charge you to keep at a moderate height, for if you fly too low the damp will clog your wings, and if too high the heat will melt them. Keep near me and you will be safe." While he gave him these instructions and fitted the wings to his shoulders, the face of the father was wet with tears, and his hands trembled. He kissed the boy, not knowing that it was for the last time. Then rising on his wings he flew off, encouraging him to follow and looked back from his own flight to see how his son managed his wings. As they flew the plowman stopped his work to gaze, and the shepherd leaned on his staff and watched them, astonished at the sight, thinking they were gods who could thus cleave the air. They passed Samos and Delos on the left and Lebynthos on the right, when the boy, exulting in his career, began to leave the guidance of his companion and soar upward as if to reach heaven. The nearness of the blazing sun softened the wax that held the feathers together, and they came off. He fluttered with his arms, but no feathers remained to hold the air. While his mouth uttered cries to his father, it was submerged in the blue waters of the sea, which thenceforth was called by his name. His father cried, "Icarus, Icarus, where are you?" At last he saw the feathers floating on the water, and bitterly lamenting his own arts, he buried the body and called the land Icaria in memory of his child. Daedalus arrived safe in Sicily, where he built a temple to Apollo and hung up his wings, an offering to the god.

Daedalus was so proud of his achievements that he could not bear the idea of a rival. His sister had placed her son Perdix under his charge to be taught the mechanical arts. He was an apt scholar and gave striking evidences of ingenuity. Walking on the seashore he picked up the spine of a fish. Imitating it, he took a piece of iron and notched it on

Anthony van Dyck, *Daedalus and Icarus,* **c. 1615, oil on canvas, Art Gallery of Ontario** (Google Cultural Institute)

CASTOR AND POLLUX

Castor and Pollux were the offspring of Leda and the Swan, under which disguise Jupiter had concealed himself. Leda gave birth to an egg, from which sprang the twins. Helen, so famous afterwards as the cause of the Trojan War, was their sister. When Theseus and his friend Pirithous had carried off Helen from Sparta, the youthful heroes Castor and Pollux, with their followers, hastened to her rescue. Theseus was absent from Attica, and the brothers were successful in recovering their sister. Castor was famous for taming and managing horses and Pollux for skill in boxing. They were united by the warmest affection, and inseparable in all their enterprises. They accompanied the Argonautic expedition. During the voyage a storm arose, and Orpheus prayed to the Samothracian gods and played on his harp, whereupon the storm ceased and stars appeared on the heads of the brothers. From this incident, Castor and Pollux came afterwards to be considered the patron deities of seamen and voyagers. (One of the ships in which St. Paul sailed was named the Castor and Pollux. See Acts 28:2.) The lambent flames, which in certain states of the atmosphere play round the sails and masts of vessels, were called by their names. After the Argonautic expedition, we find Castor and Pollux engaged in a war with Idas and Lynceus. Castor was slain, and Pollux, inconsolable for the loss of his brother, besought Jupiter to be permitted to give his own life as a ransom for him. Jupiter so far consented as to allow the two brothers to enjoy the boon of life alternately, passing one day under the earth and the next in the heavenly abodes. According to another form of the story, Jupiter rewarded the attachment of the brothers by placing them among the stars as Gemini, the Twins. They received divine honors under the name of Dioscuri (sons of Jove). They were believed to have appeared occasionally in later times, taking part with one side or the other, in hard-fought fields, and were said on such occasions to be mounted on magnificent white steeds. Thus, in the early history of Rome, they are said to have assisted the Romans at the battle of Lake Regillus, and after the victory a temple was erected in their honor on the spot where they appeared.

the edge, thus inventing the saw. He put two pieces of iron together, connecting them at one end with a rivet, and, sharpening the other ends, made a pair of compasses. Daedalus was so envious of his nephew's performances that he took an opportunity, when they were together one day on the top of a high tower, to push him off. But Minerva, who favors ingenuity, saw him falling and arrested his fate by changing him into a bird called after his name, the partridge. This bird does not build his nest in the trees, nor take lofty flights, but nestles in the hedges, and mindful of his fall, avoids high places.

CHAPTER XIV:
BACCHUS. ARIADNE.

Nicolas Poussin, *The Triumph of Bacchus,* c.1635, oil on canvas, Nelson-Atkins Museum of Art

BACCHUS

Bacchus was the son of Jupiter and Semele. Juno, to gratify her resentment against Semele, contrived a plan for her destruction. Assuming the form of Beroe, her aged nurse, she insinuated doubts whether it was indeed Jove himself who came as a lover. Heaving a sigh, she said, "I hope it will turn out so, but I can't help being afraid. People are not always what they pretend to be. If he is indeed Jove, make him give some proof of it. Ask him to come arrayed in all his splendor, such as he wears in heaven. That will put the matter beyond a doubt." Semele was persuaded to try the experiment. She asks a favor, without naming what it is. Jove gives his promise and confirms it with the irrevocable oath, attesting the river Styx, terrible to the gods themselves. Then she made known her request. The god would have stopped her as she spoke, but she was too quick for him. The words escaped, and he could neither unsay his promise nor her request. In deep distress he left her and returned to the upper regions. There he clothed himself in his splendor, not putting on all his terrors, as when he overthrew the giants, but what is known among the gods as his lesser panoply. Arrayed in this he entered the chamber of Semele. Her mortal frame could not endure the splendors of the immortal radiance. She was consumed to ashes. Jove took the infant Bacchus and gave him in charge to the Nysaean nymphs, who nourished his infancy and childhood, and for their care were rewarded by Jupiter by being placed, as the Hyades, among the stars. When Bacchus grew up he discovered the culture of the vine and the mode of extracting its precious juice; but Juno struck him with madness, and drove him forth a wanderer through various parts of the earth. In Phrygia the goddess Rhea cured him and taught him her religious rites, and he set out on a progress through Asia teaching the people the cultivation of the vine. The most famous part of his wanderings is his expedition to India, which is said to have lasted several years.

Returning in triumph he undertook to introduce his worship into Greece but was opposed by some princes who dreaded its introduction on account of the disorders and madness it brought with it. As he approached his native city Thebes, Pentheus the king, who had no respect for the new worship, forbade its rites to be performed. But when it was known that Bacchus was advancing, men and women, but chiefly the latter, young and old poured forth to meet him and to join his triumphal march. It was in vain Pentheus remonstrated, commanded, and threatened. "Go," said he to his attendants, "seize this vagabond leader of the rout and bring him to me. I will soon make him confess his false claim of heavenly parentage and renounce his counterfeit worship." It was in vain his nearest friends and wisest counselors remonstrated and begged him not to oppose the god. Their remonstrances only made him more violent. But now the attendants returned whom he had dispatched to seize Bacchus. They had been driven away by the Bacchanals but had succeeded in taking one of them prisoner, whom, with his hands tied behind him, they brought before the king. Pentheus beholding him, with wrathful countenance said, "Fellow! You shall speedily be put to death, that your fate may be a warning to others; but though I grudge the delay of your punishment, speak, tell us who you are, and what are these new rites you presume to celebrate." The prisoner unterrified responded, "My name is Acetes; my country is Maeonia; my parents were poor people, who had no fields or flocks to leave me, but they left me their fishing rods and nets and their fisherman's trade. This I followed for some time, until growing weary of remaining in one place, I learned the pilot's art and how to guide my course by the stars. It happened as I was sailing for Delos, we touched at the island of Dia and went ashore. Next morning I sent the men for fresh water and myself mounted the hill to observe the wind; when my men returned bringing with them a prize, as they thought, a boy of delicate appearance, whom they had found asleep. They judged he was a noble youth, perhaps a king's son, and they might get a liberal ransom for him. I observed his dress, his walk, his face. There was something in them which I felt sure was more than mortal. I said to my men, 'What god there is concealed in that form I know not, but some one there certainly is. Pardon us, gentle deity, for the violence we have done you, and give success to

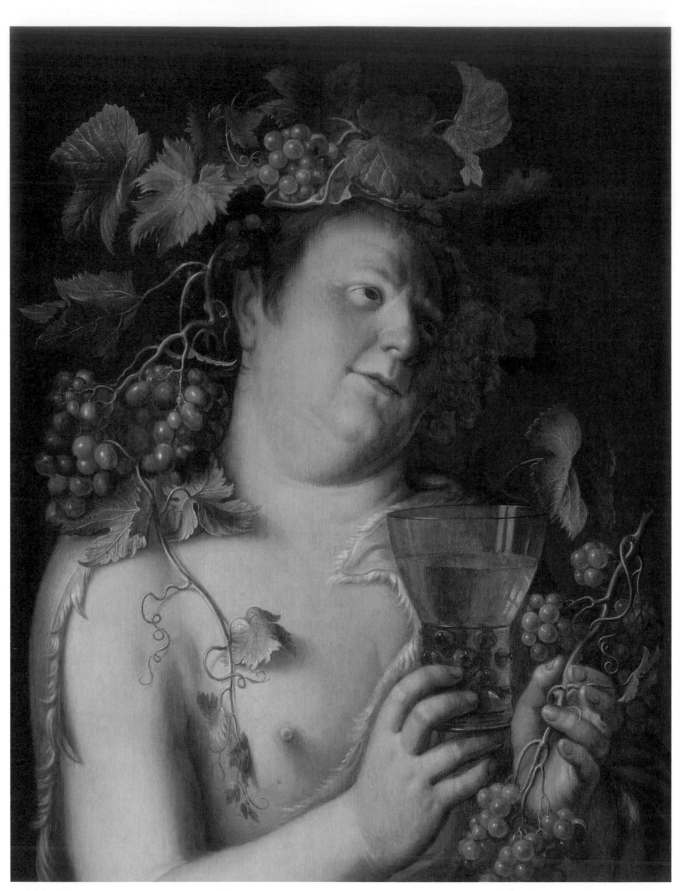

Joachim Wtewael, *Bacchus,* c. 1638, oil on panel

our undertakings.' Dictys, one of my best hands for climbing the mast and coming down by the ropes, and Melanthus, my steersman, and Epopeus the leader of the sailors' cry, one and all exclaimed, 'Spare your prayers for us.' So blind is the lust of gain! When they proceeded to put him on board I resisted them. 'This ship shall not be profaned by such impiety,' said I. 'I have a greater share in her than any of you.' But Lycabas, a turbulent fellow, seized me by the throat and attempted to throw me overboard, and I scarcely saved myself by clinging to the ropes. The rest approved the deed. Then Bacchus, for it was indeed he, as if shaking off his drowsiness, exclaimed, 'What are you doing with me? What is this fighting about? Who brought me here? Where are you going to carry me?' One of them replied, 'Fear nothing; tell us where you wish to go and we will take you there.' 'Naxos is my home,' said Bacchus; 'take me there and you shall be well rewarded.' They promised so to do, and told me to pilot the ship to Naxos. Naxos lay to the right, and I was trimming the sails to carry us there, when some by signs and others by whispers signified to me their will that I should sail in the opposite direction, and take the boy to Egypt to sell him for a slave. I was confounded and said, 'Let some one else pilot the ship,' withdrawing myself from any further agency in their wickedness. They cursed me, and one of them exclaiming, 'Don't flatter yourself that we depend on you for our safety,' took my place as pilot and bore away from Naxos.

"Then the god, pretending that he had just become aware of their treachery, looked out over the sea and said in a voice of weeping, 'Sailors, these are not the shores you promised to take me to; yonder island is not my home. What have I done that you should treat me so? It is small glory you will gain by cheating a poor boy.' I wept to hear him, but the crew laughed at both of us, and sped the vessel fast over the sea. All at once, strange as it may seem, it is true, the vessel stopped, in the mid sea, as fast as if it was fixed on the ground. The men, astonished, pulled at their oars, and spread more sail, trying to make progress by the aid of both, but all in vain. Ivy twined round the oars and hindered their motion and clung with its heavy clusters of berries to the sails. A vine, laden with grapes, ran up the mast, and along the sides of the vessel. The sound of flutes was heard and the odor of fragrant wine spread all around. The god himself had a chaplet of vine leaves and bore in his hand a spear wreathed with ivy. Tigers crouched at his feet, and lynxes and spotted panthers played around him. The sailors were seized with terror or madness; some leaped overboard; others, preparing to do the same, beheld their companions in the water undergoing a change, their bodies becoming flattened and ending in a crooked tail. One exclaimed, 'What miracle is this!' and as he spoke his mouth widened, his nostrils expanded, and scales covered all his body. Another endeavoring to pull the oar felt his hands shrink up, and presently to be no longer hands but fins; another trying to raise his arms to a rope found he had no arms, and curving his mutilated body, jumped into the sea. What had been his legs became the two ends of a crescent-shaped tail. The whole crew became dolphins and swam about the ship, now upon the surface, now under it, scattering the spray, and spouting the water from their broad nostrils. Of twenty men I alone was left. The god cheered me, as I trembled with fear. 'Fear not,' said he; 'steer toward Naxos.' I obeyed, and when we arrived there, I kindled the altars and celebrated the sacred rites of Bacchus." Pentheus here exclaimed, "We have wasted time enough on this silly story. Take him away and have him executed without delay." Acetes was led away by the attendants and shut up fast in prison; but while they were getting ready the instruments of execution, the prison doors opened of their own accord and the chains fell from his limbs, and when the guards looked for him he was no where to be found.

Pentheus would take no warning, but instead of sending others, determined to go himself to the scene of the solemnities. The mountain Cithaeron was all alive with worshippers, and the cries of the Bacchanals resounded on every side. The noise roused the anger of Pentheus as the sound of a trumpet does the fire of a warhorse. He penetrated the wood and reached an open space where the wildest scene of the orgies met his eyes. At the same moment the women saw him; and first among them his own mother, Agave, blinded by the god, cried out, "See there the wild boar, the hugest monster that prowls in these woods! Come on, sisters! I will be the first to strike the wild boar." The whole band rushed upon him, and while he now talks less arrogantly, now excuses himself, and now confesses his crime and implores pardon, they press upon and wound him. In vain he cries to his aunts to protect him from his mother. Autonoe seized one arm, Ino the other, and between them he was torn to pieces, while his mother shouted, "Victory! Victory! We have done it; the glory is ours!" So the worship of Bacchus was established in Greece.

ARIADNE

We have seen in the story of Theseus how Ariadne, the daughter of King Minos, after helping Theseus to escape from the labyrinth, was carried by him to the island of Naxos and was left there asleep, while Theseus pursued his way home without her. Ariadne, on waking and finding herself deserted, abandoned herself to grief. But Venus took pity on her and consoled her with the promise that she should have an immortal lover, instead of the mortal one she had lost. The island where Ariadne was left was the favorite island of Bacchus, the same that he wished the Tyrrhenian mariners to carry him to, when they so treacherously attempted to make prize of him. As Ariadne sat lamenting her fate, Bacchus found her, consoled her and made her his wife as Minerva had prophesied to Theseus. As a marriage present he gave her a golden crown, enriched with gems, and when she died, he took her crown and threw it up into the sky. As it mounted the gems grew brighter and were turned into stars, and preserving its form Ariadne's crown remains fixed in the heavens as a constellation, between the kneeling Hercules and the man who holds the serpent.

CHAPTER XV: ALCESTIS. ANTIGONE. PENELOPE.

ADMETUS AND ALCESTIS

Aesculapius, the son of Apollo, was endowed by his father with such skill in the healing art that he even restored the dead to life. At this Pluto took alarm and prevailed on Jupiter to launch a thunderbolt at Aesculapius. Apollo was indignant at the destruction of his son and wreaked his vengeance on the innocent workmen who had made the thunderbolt. These were the Cyclopes, who have their workshop under Mount Aetna, from which the smoke and flames of their furnaces are constantly issuing. Apollo shot his arrows at the Cyclopes, which so incensed Jupiter that he condemned him as a punishment to become the servant of a mortal for the space of one year. Accordingly Apollo went into the service of Admetus, king of Thessaly, and pastured his flocks for him on the verdant banks of the river Amphrysus. Admetus was a suitor, with others, for the hand of Alcestis, the daughter of Pelias, who promised her to him who should come for her in a chariot drawn by lions and boars. This task Admetus performed by the assistance of his divine herdsman, and was made happy in the possession of Alcestis. But Admetus fell ill, and being near to death, Apollo prevailed on the Fates to spare him on condition that some one would consent to die in his stead. Admetus, in his joy at this reprieve, thought little of the ransom, and perhaps remembering the declarations of attachment that he had often heard from his courtiers and dependents, fancied that it would be easy to find a substitute. But it was not so. Brave warriors, who would willingly have imperiled their lives for their prince, shrunk from the thought of dying for him on the bed of sickness; and old servants who had experienced his bounty and that of his house from their childhood up, were not willing to lay down the scanty remnant of their days to show their gratitude. Men asked, "Why does not one of his parents do it? They cannot in the course of nature live much longer, and who can feel like them the call to rescue the life they gave from an untimely end?" But the parents, distressed though they were at the thought of losing him, shrunk from the call. Then Alcestis, with a generous self-devotion, proffered herself as the substitute. Admetus, fond as he was of life, would not have submitted to receive it at such a cost; but there was no remedy. The condition imposed by the Fates had been met, and the decree was irrevocable. Alcestis sickened as Admetus revived, and she was rapidly sinking to the grave. Just at this time Hercules arrived at the palace of Admetus, and found all the inmates in great distress for the impending loss of the devoted wife and beloved mistress. Hercules, to whom no labor was too arduous, resolved to attempt her rescue. He went and lay in wait at the door of the chamber of the dying queen, and when Death came for his prey, he seized him and forced him to resign his victim. Alcestis recovered, and was restored to her husband.

ANTIGONE

The poems and histories of legendary Greece often relate, as has been seen, to women and their lives. Antigone was as bright an example of filial and sisterly fidelity as was Alcestis of connubial devotion. She was the daughter of Oedipus and Jocasta, who, with all their descendants, were the victims of an unrelenting fate, dooming them to destruction. Oedipus in his madness had torn out his eyes, and was driven forth from his kingdom Thebes, dreaded and abandoned by all men, as an object of divine vengeance. Antigone, his daughter, alone shared his wanderings, and remained with him until he died, and then returned to Thebes. Her brothers, Eteocles and Polynices, had agreed to share the kingdom between them and reign alternately year by year. The first year fell to the lot of Eteocles, who, when his time expired, refused to surrender the kingdom to his brother. Polynices fled to Adrastus, king of Argos, who gave him his daughter in marriage, and aided him with an army to enforce his claim to the kingdom. This led to the celebrated expedition of the "Seven against Thebes," which furnished ample materials for the epic and tragic poets of Greece. Amphiaraus, the brother-in-law of Adrastus, opposed the enterprise, for he was a soothsayer, and knew by his art that no one of the leaders except Adrastus would live to return. But Amphiaraus, on his marriage to Eriphyle, the king's sister, had agreed that whenever he and Adrastus should differ in opinion, the decision should be left to Eriphyle. Polynices, knowing this, gave Eriphyle the collar of Harmonia, and thereby gained her to his interest. This collar or necklace was a present that Vulcan had given to Harmonia on her marriage with Cadmus, and Polynices had taken it with him on his flight from Thebes. Eriphyle could not resist so tempting a bribe, and by her decision the war was resolved on, and Amphiaraus went to his cer-

Nikiphorus Lytras, *Antigone in front of the Dead Polynices*, 1865, oil on canvas, National Gallery of Greece

tain fate. He bore his part bravely in the contest but could not avert his destiny. Pursued by the enemy he fled along the river, when a thunderbolt launched by Jupiter opened the ground, and he, his chariot, and his charioteer, were swallowed up. It would not be in place here to detail all the acts of heroism or atrocity that marked the contest; but we must not omit to record the fidelity of Evadne as an offset to the weakness of Eriphyle. Capaneus, the husband of Evadne, in the ardor of the fight, declared that he would force his way into the city in spite of Jove himself. Placing a ladder against the wall, he mounted, but Jupiter, offended at his impious language, struck him with a thunderbolt. When his obsequies were celebrated, Evadne cast herself on his funeral pile and perished.

Early in the contest Eteocles consulted the soothsayer Tiresias as to the issue. Tiresias, in his youth, had by chance seen Minerva bathing. The goddess in her wrath deprived him of his sight, but afterwards relenting gave him in compensation the knowledge of future events. When consulted by Eteocles, he declared that victory should fall to Thebes if Menoeceus, the son of Creon, gave himself as a voluntary victim. The heroic youth, learning the response, threw away his life in the first encounter. The siege continued long, with varying success. At length both hosts agreed that the brothers should decide their quarrel by single combat. They fought and fell by each other's hands. The armies then renewed the fight, and at last the invaders were forced to yield, and fled, leaving their dead unburied. Creon, the uncle of the fallen princes, now become king, caused Eteocles to be buried with distinguished honor but suffered the body of Polynices to lie where it fell, forbidding every one, on pain of death, to give it burial. Antigone, the sister of Polynices, heard with indignation the revolting edict that consigned her brother's body to the dogs and vultures, depriving it of those rites that were considered essential to the repose of the dead. Unmoved by the dissuading counsel of an affectionate but timid sister, and unable to procure assistance, she determined to brave the hazard and to bury

Giovanni Battista Tiepolo, *Etiocles and Polynices,* c. 1725, oil on canvas, Kunsthistorisches Museum, Vienna, Austria

the body with her own hands. She was detected in the act, and Creon gave orders that she should be buried alive, as having deliberately set at nought the solemn edict of the city. Her love, Haemon, the son of Creon, unable to avert her fate, would not survive her, and fell by his own hand. Antigone forms the subject of two fine tragedies of the Grecian poet Sophocles.

PENELOPE

Penelope is another of those mythic heroines whose beauties were rather those of character and conduct than of person. She was the daughter of Icarius, a Spartan prince. Ulysses, king of Ithaca, sought her in marriage and won her over all competitors. When the moment came for the bride to leave her father's house, Icarius, unable to bear the thoughts of parting with his daughter, tried to persuade her to remain with him, and not accompany her husband to Ithaca. Ulysses gave Penelope her choice, to stay or go with him. Penelope made no reply, but dropped her veil over her face. Icarius urged her no further, but when she was gone erected a statue to Modesty on the spot where they parted. Ulysses and Penelope had not enjoyed their union more than a year when it was interrupted by the events that called Ulysses to the Trojan War. During his long absence, and when it was doubtful whether he still lived, and highly improbable that he would ever return, Penelope was importuned by numerous suitors, from whom there seemed no refuge but in choosing one of them for her husband. Penelope, however, employed every art to gain time, still hopping for Ulysses' return. One of her arts of delay was engaging in the preparation of a robe for the funeral canopy of Laertes, her husband's father. She pledged herself to make her choice among the suitors when the robe was finished. During the day she worked at the robe, but in the night she undid the work so that it was always in process, but never done. The rest of Penelope's history will be told when we give an account of her husband's adventures.

CHAPTER XVI: ORPHEUS AND EURYDICE. ARISTAEUS.

ORPHEUS AND EURYDICE

Orpheus was the son of Apollo and the muse Calliope. He was presented by his father with a lyre and taught to play upon it, and he played to such perfection that nothing could withstand the charm of his music. Not only his fellow mortals, but wild beasts were softened by his strains, and gathering round him laid by their fierceness, and stood entranced with his lay. Nay, the very trees and rocks were sensible to the charm. The former crowded round him and the latter relaxed somewhat of their hardness, softened by his notes. Hymen had been called to bless with his presence the nuptials of Orpheus with Eurydice; but though he attended, he brought no happy omens with him. His very torch smoked and brought tears into their eyes. In coincidence with such prognostics Eurydice, shortly after her marriage, while wandering with the nymphs, her companions, was seen by the shepherd Aristaeus, who was struck with her beauty, and made advances to her. She fled, and in flying trod upon a snake in the grass, was bitten in the foot and died. Orpheus sang his grief to all who breathed the upper air, both gods and men, and finding it all unavailing resolved to seek his wife in the regions of the dead. He descended by a cave situated on the side of the promontory of Taenarus and arrived at the Stygian realm. He passed through crowds of ghosts, and presented himself before the throne of Pluto and Proserpine. Accompanying the words with the lyre, he sung, "O deities of the underworld, to whom all we who live must come, hear my words, for they are true! I come not to spy out the secrets of Tartarus, nor to try my strength against the three-headed dog with snaky hair that guards the entrance. I come to seek my wife, whose opening years the poisonous viper's fang has brought to an untimely end. Love had led me here, Love, a god all-powerful with us who dwell on the earth, and, if old traditions say true, not less so here. I implore you by these abodes full of terror, these realms of silence and uncreated things, unite again the thread of Eurydice's life. We all are destined to you, and sooner or later must pass to your domain. She too, when she shall have filled her term of life, will rightly be yours. But until then grant her to me, I beseech you. If you deny me, I cannot return alone; you shall triumph in the death of us both." As he sang these tender strains, the very ghosts shed tears. Tantalus, in spite of his thirst, stopped for a moment his efforts for water, Ixion's wheel stood still, the vulture ceased to tear the giant's liver, the daughters of Danaus rested from their task of drawing water in a sieve,

Alexandre-Auguste Hirsch, *Calliope Teaching Orpheus*, 1865, oil on canvas

102

and Sisyphus sat on his rock to listen. Then for the first time, it is said, the cheeks of the Furies were wet with tears. Proserpine could not resist, and Pluto himself gave way. Eurydice was called. She came from among the new-arrived ghosts, limping with her wounded foot. Orpheus was permitted to take her away with him on one condition, that he should not turn round to look at her until they should have reached the upper air. Under this condition they proceeded on their way, he leading, she following, through passages dark and steep, in total silence, until they had nearly reached the outlet into the cheerful upper world, when Orpheus, in a moment of forgetfulness, to assure himself that she was still following, cast a glance behind him, when instantly she was borne away. Stretching out their arms to embrace one another they grasped only the air. Dying now a second time she yet cannot reproach her husband, for how can she blame his impatience to behold her? "Farewell," she said, "a last farewell," and was hurried away, so fast that the sound hardly reached his ears. Orpheus endeavored to follow her, and besought permission to return and try once more for her release but the stern ferryman repulsed him and refused passage. Seven days he lingered about the

Jean-Baptiste-Camille Corot, *Orpheus Leading Eurydice from the Underworld,* 1861, oil on canvas, Museum of Fine Arts, Houston

brink, without food or sleep; then bitterly accusing of cruelty the powers of Erebus, he sang his complaints to the rocks and mountains, melting the hearts of tigers and moving the oaks from their stations. He held himself aloof from womankind, dwelling constantly on the recollection of his sad mischance. The Thracian maidens tried their best to captivate him, but he repulsed their advances. They bore with him as long as they could; but finding him insensible, one day, one of them, excited by the rites of Bacchus, exclaimed, "See yonder our despiser!" and threw at him her javelin. The weapon, as soon as it came within the sound of his lyre, fell harmless at his feet. So did also the stones that they threw at him. But the women raised a scream and drowned the voice of the music, and then the missiles reached him and soon were stained with his blood. The maniacs tore him limb from limb, and threw his head and his lyre into the river Hebrus, down which they floated, murmuring sad music, to which the shores responded a plaintive symphony. The Muses gathered up the fragments of his body and buried them at Libethra, where the nightingale is said to sing over his grave more sweetly than in any other part of Greece. His lyre was placed by Jupiter among the stars. His shade passed a second time to Tartarus, where he sought out his Eurydice and embraced her, with eager arms. They roam through those happy fields together now, sometimes he leads, sometimes she; and Orpheus gazes as much as he will upon her, no longer incurring a penalty for a thoughtless glance.

ARISTAEUS, THE BEEKEEPER

Man avails himself of the instincts of the inferior animals for his own advantage. Hence sprang the art of keeping bees. Honey must first have been known as a wild product, the bees building their structures in hollow trees or holes in the rocks, or any similar cavity that chance offered. Thus occasionally the carcass of a dead animal would be occupied by the bees for that purpose. It was no doubt from some such incident that the superstition arose that the bees were engendered by the decaying flesh of the animal; and Virgil, in the following story (from the *Georgics,* Book IV.1.317), shows how this supposed fact may be turned to account

for renewing the swarm when it has been lost by disease or accident. The shepherd Aristaeus, who first taught the management of bees, was the son of the water nymph Cyrene. His bees had perished, and he resorted for aid to his mother. He stood at the riverside and thus addressed her: "Oh, mother, the pride of my life is taken from me! I have lost my precious bees. My care and skill have availed me nothing, and you, my mother, have not warded off from me the blow of misfortune." His mother heard these complaints as she sat in her palace at the bottom of the river with her attendant nymphs around her. They were engaged in female occupations, spinning and weaving, while one told stories to amuse the rest. The sad voice of Aristaeus interrupting their occupation, one of them put her head above the water and seeing him, returned and gave information to his mother, who ordered that he should be brought into her presence. The river at her command opened itself and let him pass in, while it stood curled like a mountain on either side. He descended to the region where the fountains of the great rivers lie; he saw the enormous receptacles of waters and was almost deafened with the roar, while he surveyed them hurrying off in various directions to water the face of the earth. Arriving at his mother's apartment he was hospitably received by Cyrene and her nymphs, who spread their table with the richest dainties. They first poured out libations to Neptune, then regaled themselves with the feast, and after that Cyrene thus addressed him: "There is an old prophet named Proteus, who dwells in the sea and is a favorite of Neptune, whose herd of sea-calves he pastures. We nymphs hold him in great respect, for he is a learned sage, and knows all things, past, present, and to come. He can tell you, my son, the cause of the mortality among your bees, and how you may remedy it. But he will not do it voluntarily, however you may entreat him. You must compel him by force. If you seize him and chain him, he will answer your questions in order to get released, for he cannot, by all his arts, get away if you hold fast the chains. I will carry you to his cave, where he comes at noon to take his midday repose. Then you may easily secure him. But when he finds himself captured, his resort is to a power he possesses of changing himself into various forms. He will become a wild boar or a fierce tiger, a scaly dragon, or lion with yellow mane. Or he will make a noise like the crackling of flames or the rush of water, so as to tempt you to let go the chain, when he will make his escape. But you have only to keep him fast bound, and at last when he finds all his arts unavailing, he will return to his own figure and obey your commands." So saying she sprinkled her son with fragrant nectar, the beverage of the gods, and immediately an unusual vigor filled his frame and courage his heart, while perfume breathed all around him. The nymph led her son to the prophet's cave, and concealed him among the recesses of the rocks, while she herself took her place behind the clouds. Then noon came and the hour when men and herds retreat from the glaring sun to indulge in quiet slumber, Proteus issued from the water, followed by his herd of sea-calves, which spread themselves along the shore. He sat on the rock and counted his herd; then stretched himself on the floor of the cave and went to sleep. Aristaeus hardly allowed him to get fairly asleep before he fixed the fetters on him and shouted aloud. Proteus, waking and finding himself captured, immediately resorted to his arts, becoming first a fire, then a flood, then a horrible wild beast, in rapid succession. But trying all in vain, he at last resumed his own form and addressed the youth in angry accents: "Who are you, bold youth, who thus invade my abode, and what do you want with me?" Aristaeus replied, "Proteus, you know already, for it is needless for any one to attempt to deceive you. And do you also cease your efforts to elude me. I am led hither by divine assistance, to know from you the cause of my misfortune and how to remedy it." At these words the prophet, fixing on him his gray eyes with a piercing look, thus spoke: "You received the merited reward of your deeds, by which Eurydice met her death, for in flying from you she trod upon a serpent, of whose bite she died. To avenge her death the nymphs, her companions, have sent this destruction on your bees. You have to appease their anger, and thus it must be done: Select four bulls of perfect form and size, and four cows of equal beauty, build four altars to the nymphs, and sacrifice the animals, leaving their

carcasses in the leafy grove. To Orpheus and Eurydice you shall pay such funeral honors as may allay their resentment. Returning after nine days you will examine the bodies of the cattle slain and see what will befall." Aristaeus faithfully obeyed these directions. He sacrificed the cattle, he left their bodies in the grove, he offered funeral honors to the shades of Orpheus and Eurydice; then returning on the ninth day he examined the bodies of the animals, and, wonderful to relate! A swarm of bees had taken possession of one of the carcasses, and were pursuing their labors there as in a hive.

MARSYAS

Minerva invented the flute, and played upon it to the delight of all the celestial auditors; but the mischievous urchin Cupid having dared to laugh at the queer face which the goddess made while playing, Minerva threw the instrument indignantly away, and it fell down to earth, and was found by Marsyas. He blew upon it, and drew from it such ravishing sounds that he was tempted to challenge Apollo himself to a musical contest. The god of course triumphed, and punished Marsyas by flaying him alive.

MELAMPUS

Melampus was the first mortal endowed with prophetic powers. Before his house there stood an oak tree containing a serpent's nest. The old serpents were killed by the servants, but Melampus took care of the young ones and fed them carefully. One day when he was asleep under the oak, the serpents licked his ears with their tongues. On awaking he was astonished to find that he now understood the language of birds and creeping things. This knowledge enabled him to foretell future events, and he became a renowned soothsayer. At one time his enemies took him captive and kept him strictly imprisoned. Melampus in the silence of night heard the woodworms in the timbers talking together, and found out by what they said that the timbers were nearly eaten through, and the roof would soon fall in. He told his captors and demanded to be let out, warning them also. They took his warning, and thus escaped destruction, and rewarded Melampus and held him in high honor.

CHAPTER XVII: ENDYMION. ORION. AURORA AND TITHONUS. ACIS AND GALATEA.

ENDYMION

Endymion was a beautiful youth who fed his flock on Mount Latmos. One calm, clear night, Diana, the Moon, looked down and saw him sleeping. The cold heart of the virgin goddess was warmed by his surpassing beauty, and she came down to him, kissed him, and watched over him while he slept. Another story was that Jupiter bestowed on him the gift of perpetual youth united with perpetual sleep. Of one so gifted we can have but few adventures to record. Diana, it was said, took care that his fortunes should not suffer by his inactive life, for she made his flock increase and guarded his sheep and lambs from the wild beasts. The story of Endymion has a peculiar charm from the human meaning, which it so thinly veils. We see in Endymion the young poet, his fancy and his heart seeking in vain for that which can satisfy them, finding his favorite hour in the quiet moonlight, and nursing there beneath the beams of the bright and silent witness the melancholy and the ardor which consumes him. The story suggests aspiring and poetic love, a life spent more in dreams than in reality, and an early and welcome death.

ORION

Orion was the son of Neptune. He was a handsome giant and a mighty hunter. His father gave him the power of wading through the depths of the sea, or as others say, of walking on its surface. Orion loved Merope, the daughter of Oenopion, king of Chios and sought her in marriage. He cleared the island of wild beasts and brought the spoils of the chase as presents to his beloved; but as Oenopion constantly deferred his consent, Orion attempted to gain possession of the maiden by violence. Her father, incensed at this conduct, having made Orion drunk, deprived him of his sight, and cast him out on the seashore. The blinded hero followed the sound of the Cyclops' hammer until he reached Lemnos and came to the forge of Vulcan, who, taking pity on him, gave him Kedalion, one of his men, to be his guide to the abode of the sun. Placing Kedalion on his shoulders, Orion proceeded to the east, and there meeting the sun-god, was restored to sight by his beam. After this he dwelt as a hunter with Diana, with whom he was a favorite, and it is even said she was about to marry him. Her brother was highly displeased and often reproached her, but to no purpose. One day, observing Orion wading though the sea with his head just above the water, Apollo pointed it out to his sister and maintained that she could not hit that black thing on the sea. The archer-goddess discharged a shaft with fatal aim. The waves rolled the dead body of Orion to the land, and bewailing her fatal error with many tears, Diana placed him among the stars, where he appears as a giant, with a girdle, sword, lion's skin, and club. Sirius, his dog, follows him, and the Pleiads fly before him. The Pleiads were daughters of Atlas and nymphs of Diana's train. One day Orion saw them, and became enamored, and pursued them. In their distress they prayed to the gods to change their form, and Jupiter in pity turned them into pigeons and then made them a constellation in the sky. Though their number was seven, only six stars are visible, for Electra, one of them, it is said, left her place that she might not behold the ruin of Troy, for that city was founded by her son Dardanus. The sight had such an effect on her sisters that they have looked pale ever since.

AURORA AND TITHONUS.

Aurora, the goddess of the Dawn, like her sister the Moon, was at times inspired with the love of mortals. Her greatest favorite was Tithonus, son of Laomedon, king of Troy. She stole him away and prevailed on Jupiter to grant him immortality, but forgetting to have youth joined in the gift, after some time she began to discern, to her great mortification, that he was growing old. When his hair was quite white she left his society; but he still had the range of her palace, lived on ambrosial food, and was clad in celestial raiment. At length he lost the power of using his limbs, and then she shut him up in his chamber, whence his feeble voice might at times be heard. Finally she turned him into a grasshopper. Memnon was the son of Aurora and Tithonus. He was king of the Aethiopians, and dwelt in the extreme east, on the shore of Ocean. He came with his warriors to assist the kindred of his father in the war of Troy. King Priam received him with great honors and listened with admiration to his narrative of the wonders of the ocean shore. The very day after his arrival, Memnon, impatient of repose, led his troops to the field. Antilochus, the brave son of Nestor, fell by his hand, and the Greeks were put to flight, when Achilles appeared and restored the battle. A long and doubtful contest ensued between him and the son of Aurora; at length Memnon fell, and the Trojans fled in dismay. Aurora had viewed with apprehension the danger of her son. When she saw him fall directed his brothers, the Winds, to convey his body to the banks of the river Esepus in Paphlagonia. In the evening Aurora came, accompanied by the Hours and the Pleiads, and wept and lamented over her son. Night, in sympathy with her grief, spread the heaven with clouds; all nature mourned for the offspring of the Dawn. The Aethiopians raised his tomb on the banks of the stream in the grove of the nymphs, and Jupiter caused the sparks and cinders of his funeral pyre to be turned into birds, which, dividing into two flocks, fought over the pyre until they fell into the flame. Every year, at the anniversary of his death, they return and celebrate his obsequies in like manner. Aurora remains inconsolable for the loss of her son. Her tears still flow, and may be seen at early morning in the form of dewdrops on the grass. Unlike most of the marvels of ancient mythology, there will exist some memorials of this. On the banks of the river Nile, in Egypt, are two colossal statues, one of which is said to be the statue of Memnon. Ancient writers record that when the first rays of the rising sun fall upon this statue, a sound is heard to issue from it, which they compare to the snapping of a harp-string. There is some doubt about the identification of the existing statue with the one described by the ancients, and the mysterious sounds are still more doubtful. Yet there are not wanting some modern testimonies to their being still audible. It has been suggested that sounds produced by confined air making its escape from crevices or caverns in the rocks may have given some ground for the story. Sir Gardner Wilkinson, a late traveller, of the highest authority, examined the statue itself, and discovered that it was hollow, and that "in the lap of the statue is a stone, which, on being struck, emits a metallic sound, that might still be made use of to deceive a visitor who was predisposed to believe its powers."

ACIS AND GALATEA

Scylla was a fair virgin of Sicily, a favorite of the Sea Nymphs. She had many suitors, but repelled them all, and would go to the grotto of Galatea, and tell her how she was persecuted. One day the goddess, while Scylla dressed her hair, listened to the story, and then replied, "Yet, maiden, your persecutors are of the not ungentle race of men, whom if you will you can repel; but I, the daughter of Nereus, and protected by such a band of sisters, found no escape from the passion of the Cyclops but in the depths of the sea;" and tears stopped her utterance, which when the pitying maiden had wiped away with her delicate finger and soothed the goddess, "Tell me, dearest," said she, "the cause of your grief." Galatea then said, "Acis was the son of Faunus and a Naiad. His father and mother loved him dearly, but their love was not equal to mine. For the beautiful youth attached himself to me alone, and he was just sixteen years old, the down just beginning to darken his cheeks. As much as I sought his society, so much did the Cyclops seek mine; and if you ask me whether my love for Acis or my hatred for Polyphemus was the stronger, I cannot tell you; they were in equal measure. Oh, Venus, how great is thy power! This fierce giant, the terror of the woods, whom no hapless stranger escaped unharmed, who defied even Jove himself, learned to feel what love was, and touched with a passion for me, forgot his flocks and his well-stored caverns. Then, for the first time, he began to take some care of his appearance, and to try to make himself agreeable; he harrowed those coarse locks of his with a comb, and mowed his beard with a sickle, looked at his harsh features in the water, and composed his countenance. His love of slaughter, his fierceness and thirst of blood prevailed no more, and ships that touched at his island went away in safety. He paced up and down the seashore, imprinting huge tracks with his heavy tread, and, when weary, lay tranquilly in his cave.

"There is a cliff which projects into the sea, which washes it on either side. Thither one day the huge Cyclops ascended, and sat down while his flocks spread themselves around. Laying down his staff, which would have served for a mast to hold a vessel's sail, and taking his instrument, compacted of numerous pipes, he made the hills and the waters echo the music of his song. I lay hid under a rock, by the side of my beloved Acis and listened to the distant strain. It was full of extravagant praises of my beauty, mingled with passionate reproaches of my coldness and cruelty. When he had finished he rose up, and like a raging bull, that cannot stand still, wandered off into the woods. Acis and I thought no more of him, until on a sudden he came to a spot that gave him a view of us as we sat. 'I see you,' he exclaimed, 'and I will make this the last of your love-meetings.' His voice was a roar such as an angry Cyclops alone could utter. Aetna trembled at the sound. I, overcome with terror, plunged into the water. Acis turned and fled, crying, 'Save me, Galatea, save me, my parents!' The Cyclops pursued him and, tearing a rock from the side of the mountain, hurled it at him. Though only a corner of it touched him, it overwhelmed him. All that fate left in my power I did for Acis. I endowed him with the honors of his grandfather the river god. The purple blood flowed out from under the rock, but by degrees grew paler and looked like the stream of a river rendered turbid by rains, and in time it became clear. The rock cleaved open, and the water, as it gushed from the chasm, uttered a pleasing murmur." Thus Acis was changed into a river, and the river retains the name of Acis.

CHAPTER XVIII: THE TROJAN WAR.

Minerva was the goddess of wisdom, but on one occasion she did a very foolish thing; she entered into competition with Juno and Venus for the prize of beauty. It happened thus. At the nuptials of Peleus and Thetis all the gods were invited with the exception of Eris, or Discord. Enraged at her exclusion, the goddess threw a golden apple among the guests with the inscription, "For the most beautiful." Thereupon Juno, Venus, and Minerva, each claimed the apple. Jupiter, not willing to decide in so delicate a matter, sent the goddesses to Mount Ida, where the beautiful shepherd Paris was tending his flocks, and to him was committed the decision. The goddesses accordingly appeared before him. Juno promised him power and riches, Minerva glory and renown in war, and Venus the fairest of women for his wife, each attempting to bias his decision in her own favor. Paris decided in favor of Venus and gave her the golden apple, thus making the two other goddesses his enemies. Under the protection of Venus, Paris sailed to Greece, and was hospitably received by Menelaus, king of Sparta. Now Helen, the wife of Menelaus, was the very woman whom Venus had destined for Paris, the fairest of her sex. She had been sought as a bride by numerous suitors, and before her decision was made known, they all, at the suggestion of Ulysses, one of their number, took an oath that they would defend her from all injury and avenge her cause if necessary. She chose Menelaus, and was living with him happily when Paris became their guest. Paris, aided by Venus, persuaded her to elope with him and carried her to Troy, whence arose the famous Trojan War, the theme of the greatest poems of antiquity, those of Homer and Virgil. Menelaus called upon his brother chieftains of Greece to fulfill their pledge, and join him in his efforts to recover his wife. They generally came forward, but Ulysses, who had married Penelope and was very happy in his wife and child, had no disposition to embark in such a troublesome affair. He therefore hung back and Palamedes was sent to urge him. When Palamedes arrived at Ithaca, Ulysses pretended to be mad. He yoked an ass and an ox together to the plow and began to sow salt. Palamedes, to try him, placed the infant Telemachus before the plow, whereupon the father turned the plow aside, showing plainly that he was no madman, and after that could no longer refuse to fulfill his promise.

Being now himself gained for the undertaking, he lent his aid to bring in other reluctant chiefs, especially Achilles. This hero was the son of that Thetis at whose marriage the apple of Discord had been thrown among the goddesses. Thetis was herself one of the immortals, a sea nymph, and knowing that her son was fated to perish before Troy if he went on the expedition, she endeavored to prevent his going. She sent him away to the court of king Lycomedes, and induced him to conceal himself in the disguise of a maiden among the daughters of the king. Ulysses, hearing he was there, went disguised as a merchant to the palace and offered for sale female ornaments, among which he had placed some arms. While the king's daughters were engrossed with the other contents of the merchant's pack, Achilles handled the weapons and thereby betrayed himself to the keen eye of Ulysses, who found no great difficulty in persuading him to disregard his mother's prudent counsels and join his countrymen in the war.

Priam was king of Troy, and Paris, the shepherd and seducer of Helen, was his son. Paris had been brought up in obscurity, because there were certain ominous forebodings connected with him from his infancy that he would be the ruin of the state. These forebodings seemed at length likely to be realized, for the Grecian armament now in preparation was the greatest that had ever been fitted out. Agamemnon, king of Mycenae, and brother of the injured Menelaus, was chosen commander-in-chief. Achilles was their most illustrious warrior. After him ranked Ajax, gigantic in size and of great courage, but dull of intellect, Diomedes, second only to Achilles in all the qualities of a hero, Ulysses, famous for his sagacity, and Nestor, the oldest of the Grecian chiefs, and one to whom they all looked up for counsel. But Troy was no feeble enemy. Priam, the king, was now old, but he had been a wise prince and had strengthened his state by good government at home and numerous alliances with his neighbors. But the principal stay and support of his throne was his son Hector, one of the noblest characters painted by heathen antiquity. Hector felt, from the first, a presentiment of the fall of his country, but still persevered in his heroic resistance, yet by no means justified the wrong that brought this danger upon her. He was united in marriage with Andromache, and as a husband and father his character was not less admirable than as a warrior. The principal leaders on the side of the Trojans, besides Hector, were Aeneas and Deiphobus, Glaucus and Sarpedon. After two years of preparation the Greek fleet and army assembled in the port of Aulis in Boeotia. Here Agamemnon in hunting killed a stag sacred to Diana, and the goddess in return visited the army with pestilence and produced a calm that prevented the ships from leaving the port. Calchas the soothsayer thereupon announced that the wrath of the virgin goddess could only be appeased by the sacrifice of a virgin on her altar, and

Niklaus Manuel , *The Judgment of Paris,* c. 1520, Tempera on canvas, Kunstmuseum, Basel

that none other but the daughter of the offender would be acceptable. Agamemnon, however reluctant, yielded his consent, and the maiden Iphigenia was sent for under the pretense that she was to be married to Achilles. When she was about to be sacrificed the goddess relented and snatched her away, leaving a hind in her place, and Iphigenia enveloped in a cloud was carried to Tauris, where Diana made her priestess of her temple.

The wind now proving fair the fleet made sail and brought the forces to the coast of Troy. The Trojans came to oppose their landing, and at the first onset Protesilaus fell by the hand of Hector. Protesilaus had left at home his wife Laodamia, who was most tenderly attached to him. When the news of his death reached her she implored the gods to be allowed to converse with him for only three hours. The request was granted. Mercury led Protesilaus back to the upper world, and when he died a second time Laodamia died with him. There was a story that the nymphs planted elm trees round his grave that grew until they were high enough to command a view of Troy, and then withered away, while fresh branches sprang from the roots.

THE ILIAD

The war continued without decisive results for nine years. Then an event occurred which seemed likely to be fatal to the cause of the Greeks, and that was a quarrel between Achilles and Agamemnon. It is at this point that the great poem of Homer, the *Iliad,* begins. The Greeks, though unsuccessful against Troy, had taken the neighboring and allied cities, and in the division of the spoil a female captive, by name Chryseis, daughter of Chryses, priest of Apollo, had fallen to the share of Agamemnon. Chryses came bearing the sacred emblems of his office and begged the release of his daughter. Agamemnon refused. Thereupon Chryses implored Apollo to afflict the Greeks until they should be forced to yield their prey. Apollo granted the prayer of his priest and sent pestilence into the Grecian camp. Then a council was called to deliberate how to allay the wrath of the gods and avert the plague. Achilles boldly charged their misfortunes upon Agamemnon as caused by his withholding Chryseis. Agamemnon enraged, consented to relinquish his captive but demanded that Achilles should yield to him in her stead Briseis, a maiden who had fallen to Achilles' share in the division of the spoil. Achilles submitted but forthwith declared that he would take no further part in the war. He withdrew his forces from the general camp and openly avowed his intention of returning home to Greece. The gods and goddesses interested themselves as much in this famous war as the parties themselves. It was well known to them that fate had decreed that Troy should fall, at last, if her enemies should persevere and not voluntarily abandon the enterprise. Yet there was room enough left for chance to excite by turns the hopes and fears of the powers above who took part with either side. Juno and Minerva, in consequence of the slight put upon their charms by Paris, were hostile to the Trojans; Venus for the opposite cause favored them. Venus enlisted her admirer Mars on the same side, but Neptune favored the Greeks. Apollo was neutral, sometimes taking one side, sometimes the other, and Jove himself, though he loved the good King Priam, yet exercised a degree of impartiality; not however without exceptions. Thetis, the mother of Achilles, warmly resented the injury done to her son. She repaired immediately to Jove's palace, and besought him to make the Greeks repent of their injustice to Achilles by granting success to the Trojan arms. Jupiter consented; and in the battle that ensued the Trojans were completely successful. The Greeks were driven from the field and took refuge in their ships.

Then Agamemnon called a council of his wisest and bravest chiefs. Nestor advised that an embassy should be sent to Achilles to persuade him to return to the field; that Agamemnon should yield the maiden, the cause of the dispute, with ample gifts to atone for the wrong he had done. Agamemnon consented, and Ulysses, Ajax, and Phoenix were sent to carry to Achilles the penitent message. They performed that duty, but Achilles was deaf to their entreaties. He positively refused to return to the field and persisted in his resolution to embark for Greece without delay. The Greeks had constructed a rampart around their ships, and now, instead of besieging Troy, they were in a manner besieged themselves within their rampart. The next day after the unsuccessful embassy to Achilles, a battle was fought, and the Trojans, favored by Jove, were successful, and succeeded in forcing a passage through the Grecian rampart, and were about to set fire to the ships. Neptune, seeing the Greeks so pressed, came to their rescue. He appeared in the form of Calchas the prophet, encouraged the warriors with his shouts, and appealed to each individually until he raised their ardor to such a pitch that they forced the Trojans to give way. Ajax performed prodigies of valor, and at length encountered Hector. Ajax shouted defiance, to which Hector replied, and hurled his lance at the huge warrior. It was well aimed, and struck Ajax where the belts that bore his sword and shield crossed each other

Achilles' Surrender of Briseis, 1st century CE, Fresco, Naples National Archaeological Museum on the breast. The double guard prevented its penetrating, and it fell harmless. Then Ajax, seeing a huge stone, one of those that served to prop the ships, hurled it at Hector. It struck him in the neck and stretched him on the plain. His followers instantly seized him and bore him off stunned and wounded.

While Neptune was thus aiding the Greeks and driving back the Trojans, Jupiter saw nothing of what was going on, for his attention had been drawn from the field by the wiles of Juno. That goddess had arrayed herself in all her charms, and, to crown all, had borrowed of Venus her girdle called Cestus, which had the effect to heighten the wearer's charms to such a degree that they were quite irresistible. So prepared, Juno went to join her husband, who sat on Olympus watching the battle. When he beheld her she looked so charming that the fondness of his early love revived, and, forgetting the contending armies and all other affairs of state, he thought only of her and let the battle go as it would. But this absorption did not continue long, and when, upon turning his eyes downward, he beheld Hector stretched on the plain almost lifeless from pain and bruises, he dismissed Juno in a rage, commanding her to send Iris and Apollo to him. When Iris came, he sent her with a stern message to Neptune, ordering him instantly to quit the field. Apollo was dispatched to heal Hector's bruises and to inspirit his heart. These orders were obeyed with such speed that while the battle still raged, Hector returned to the field and Neptune betook himself to his own dominions. An arrow from Paris's bow wounded Machaon, son of Aesculapius, who inherited his father's art of healing, and was therefore of great value to the Greeks as their surgeon, besides being one of their bravest warriors. Nestor took Machaon in his chariot and conveyed him from the field. As they passed the ships of Achilles, that hero, looking out over the field, saw the chariot of Nestor and recognized the old chief, but could not discern who the wounded chief was. So calling Patroclus, his companion and dearest friend, he sent him to Nestor's tent to inquire. Patroclus, arriving at Nestor's tent, saw Machaon wounded, and having told the cause of his coming would have hastened away, but Nestor detained him, to tell him the extent of the Grecian calamities. He reminded him also how, at the time of departing for Troy, Achilles and himself had been charged by their respective fathers with different advice; Achilles to aspire to the highest pitch of glory, Patroclus, as the elder, to keep watch over his friend, and to guide his inexperience. "Now," said Nestor, "is the time for such influence. If the gods so please, thou mayest win him back to the common cause; but if not let him at least send his soldiers to the field, and come thou, Patroclus, clad in his armor, and perhaps the very sight of it may drive back the Trojans." Patroclus was strongly moved with this address, and hastened back to Achilles, revolving in his mind all he had seen and heard. He told the prince the sad condition of affairs at the camp of their late associates; Diomedes, Ulysses, Agamemnon, Machaon, all wounded, the rampart broken down, the enemy among the ships preparing to burn them, and thus to cut off all means of return to Greece. While they spoke the flames burst forth from one of the ships. Achilles, at the sight, relented so far as to grant Patroclus his request to lead the Myrmidons (for so were Achilles' soldiers called) to the field, and to lend him his armor that he might thereby strike more terror into the minds of the Trojans. Without delay the soldiers were marshaled, Patroclus put on the radiant armor and mounted the chariot of Achilles and led forth the men ardent for battle. But before he went, Achilles strictly charged him that he should be content with repelling the foe. "Seek not," said he, "to press the Trojans without me, lest thou add still more to the disgrace already mine." Then exhorting the troops to do their best he dismissed them full of ardor to the fight. Patroclus and his Myrmidons at once plunged into the contest where it raged hottest; at the sight of which the joyful Grecians shouted and the ships reechoed the acclaim. The Trojans, at the sight of the well-known armor, struck with terror, looked everywhere for refuge. First those who had got possession of the ship and set it on fire left and allowed the Grecians to retake it and extinguish the flames. Then the rest of the Trojans

Benjamin West, *Thetis Bringing Armor to Achilles,* 1806, oil on canvas, New Britain Museum of Art, New Britain, Connecticut

fled in dismay. Ajax, Menelaus, and the two sons of Nestor performed prodigies of valor. Hector was forced to turn his horses' heads and retire from the enclosure, leaving his men entangled in the fosse to escape as they could. Patroclus drove them before him, slaying many, none daring to make a stand against him. At last Sarpedon, son of Jove, ventured to oppose himself in fight to Patroclus. Jupiter looked down upon him and would have snatched him from the fate that awaited him, but Juno hinted that if he did so it would induce all others of the inhabitants of heaven to interpose in like manner whenever any of their offspring were endangered; to which reason Jove yielded. Sarpedon threw his spear but missed Patroclus, but Patroclus threw his with better success. It pierced Sarpedon's breast and he fell, and, calling to his friends to save his body from the foe, expired. Then a furious contest arose for the possession of the corpse. The Greeks succeeded and stripped Sarpedon of his armor; but Jove would not allow the remains of his son to be dishonored, and by his command Apollo snatched from the midst of the combatants the body of Sarpedon and committed it to the care of the twin brothers Death and Sleep, by whom it was transported to Lycia, the native land of Sarpedon, where it received due funeral rites.

Thus far Patroclus had succeeded to his utmost wish in repelling the Trojans and relieving his countrymen, but now came a change of fortune. Hector, borne in his chariot, confronted him. Patroclus threw a vast stone at Hector, which missed its aim, but smote Cebriones, the charioteer, and knocked him from the car. Hector leaped from the chariot to rescue his friend, and Patroclus also descended to complete his victory. Thus the two heroes met face to face. At this decisive moment the poet, as if reluctant to give Hector the glory, records that Phoebus took part against Patroclus. He struck the helmet from his head and the lance from his hand. At the same moment an obscure Trojan wounded him in the back, and Hector pressing forward pierced him with his spear. He fell mortally wounded. Then arose a tremendous conflict for the body of Patroclus, but his armor was at once taken possession of by Hector, who, retiring a short distance, divested himself of his own armor and put on that of Achilles, then returned to the fight. Ajax and Menelaus defended the body, and Hector and his bravest warriors struggled to capture it. The battle raged with equal fortune, when Jove enveloped the whole face of heaven with a dark cloud. The lightning flashed, the thunder roared, and Ajax, looking round for some one whom he might dispatch to Achilles to tell him of the death of his friend and of the imminent danger that his remains would fall into the hands of the enemy, could see no suitable messenger. It was then that he exclaimed in those famous lines so often quoted, "Father of heaven and earth! Deliver thou Achaia's host from darkness; clear the skies; Give day; and, since thy sovereign will is such, Destruction with it; but, oh, give us day." Jupiter heard the prayer and dispersed the clouds. Then Ajax sent Antilochus to Achilles with the intelligence of Patroclus's death, and of the conflict raging for his remains. The Greeks at last succeeded in bearing off the body to the ships, closely pursued by Hector and Aeneas and rest of the Trojans. Achilles heard the fate of his friend with such distress that Antilochus feared for a while that he would destroy himself. His groans reached the ears of his mother, Thetis, far down in the deeps of ocean where she abode, and she hastened to him to inquire the cause. She found him overwhelmed with self-reproach that he had indulged his resentment so far and suffered his friend to fall a victim to it. But his only consolation was the hope of revenge. He would fly instantly in search of Hector. But his mother reminded him that he was now without armor, and promised him, if he would but wait until the morrow, she would procure for him a suit of armor from Vulcan more than equal to that he had lost. He consented, and Thetis immediately repaired to Vulcan's palace.

She found him busy at his forge making tripods for his own use, so artfully constructed that they moved forward of their own accord when wanted, and retired again when dismissed. On hearing the request of Thetis, Vulcan immediately laid aside his work and hastened to comply with her wishes. He fabricated a splendid suit of armor for Achilles, first a shield adorned with elaborate devices, then a helmet crested with gold, then a corselet and greaves of impenetrable temper, all perfectly adapted to his form, and of consummate workmanship. It was all done in one night, and Thetis, receiving it, descended with it to earth and laid it down at Achilles' feet at the dawn of day. The first glow of pleasure that Achilles had felt since the death of Patroclus was at the sight of this splendid armor. And now arrayed in it, he went forth into the camp, calling all the chiefs to council. When they were all assembled he addressed them. Renouncing his displeasure against Agamemnon and bitterly lamenting the miseries that had resulted from it, he called on them to proceed at once to the field. Agamemnon made a suitable reply, laying all the blame on Ate, the goddess of discord, and thereupon complete reconcilement took place between the heroes. Then Achilles went forth to battle, inspired with a rage and thirst for vengeance that made him irresistible. The bravest warriors fled before him or fell by his lance. Hector, cautioned by Apollo, kept aloof, but the god, assuming the form of one of Priam's sons, Lycaon,

Franz von Matsch, *The Triumph of Achilles,* fresco from the Achilleion in Corfu, Greece

urged Aeneas to encounter the terrible warrior. Aeneas, though he felt himself unequal, did not decline the combat. He hurled his spear with all his force against the shield, the work of Vulcan. It was formed of five metal plates; two were of brass, two of tin, and one of gold. The spear pierced two thicknesses, but was stopped in the third. Achilles threw his with better success. It pierced through the shield of Aeneas, but glanced near his shoulder and made no wound. Then Aeneas seized a stone, such as two men of modern times could hardly lift, and was about to throw it, and Achilles, with sword drawn, was about to rush upon him, when Neptune, who looked out upon the contest, moved with pity for Aeneas, who he saw would surely fall a victim if not speedily rescued, spread a cloud between the combatants, and lifting Aeneas from the ground, bore him over the heads of warriors and steeds to the rear of the battle. Achilles, when the mist cleared away, looked round in vain for his adversary, and acknowledging the prodigy, turned his arms against other champions. But none dared stand before him, and Priam looking down from his city walls beheld his whole army in full flight towards the city. He gave command to open wide the gates to receive the fugitives, and to shut them as soon as the Trojans should have passed, lest the enemy should enter likewise. But Achilles was so close in pursuit that that would have been impossible if Apollo had not, in the form of Agenor, Priam's son, encountered Achilles for a while, then turned to fly, and taken the way apart from the city. Achilles pursued and had chased his supposed victim far from the walls, when Apollo disclosed himself, and Achilles, perceiving how he had been deluded, gave up the chase. But when the rest had escaped into the town Hector stood without, determined to await the combat. His old father called to him from the walls and begged him to retire nor tempt the encounter. His mother, Hecuba, also besought him to the same effect, but all in vain. "How can I," said he to himself, "by whose command the people went to this day's contest, where so many have fallen, seek safety for myself against a single foe? But what if I offer him to yield up Helen and all her treasures and ample of our own beside? Ah no! It is too late. He would not even hear me through, but slay me while I spoke." While he thus ruminated, Achilles approached, terrible as Mars, his armor flashing lighting as he moved. At that sight Hector's heart failed him and he fled. Achilles swiftly pursued. They ran, still keeping near the walls, until they had thrice encircled the city. As often as Hector approached the walls Achilles intercepted him and forced him to keep out in a wider circle. But Apollo sustained Hector's strength, and would not let him sink in weariness. Then Pallas, assuming the form of Deiphobus, Hector's bravest brother, appeared suddenly at his side. Hector saw him with delight, and, thus strengthened, stopped his flight and turned to meet Achilles. Hector threw his spear, which struck the shield of Achilles and bounded back. He turned to receive another from the hand of Deiphobus, but Deiphobus was gone. Then Hector understood his doom and said, "Alas! It is plain this is my hour to die! I thought Deiphobus at hand, but Pallas deceived me, and he is still in Troy. But I will not fall inglorious." So saying, he drew his falchion from his side and rushed at once to combat. Achilles, secured behind his shield, waited the approach of Hector. When he came within reach of his spear, Achilles, choosing with his eye a vulnerable part where the armor leaves the neck uncovered, aimed his spear at that part, and Hector fell, death-wounded, and feebly said, "Spare my body! Let my parents ransom it, and let me receive funeral rites from the sons and daughters of Troy." To which Achilles replied, "Dog, name not ransom nor pity to me, on whom you have brought such dire distress. No! Trust me, nought shall save thy carcass from the dogs. Though twenty ransoms and thy weight in gold were offered, I would refuse it all." So saying, he stripped the body of its armor, and fastening cords to the feet, tied them behind his chariot, leaving the body to trail along the ground. Then mounting the chariot he lashed the steeds, and so dragged the body to and fro before the city. What words can tell the grief of King Priam and Queen Hecuba at this sight! His people could scarce restrain the old king from rushing forth. He threw himself in the dust, and besought them each by name to give him way. Hecuba's distress was not less violent. The citizens stood round them weeping. The sound

of the mourning reached the ears of Andromache, the wife of Hector, as she sat among her maidens at work, and anticipating evil she went forth to the wall. When she saw the sight there presented, she would have thrown herself headlong from the wall, but fainted and fell into the arms of her maidens. Recovering, she bewailed her fate, picturing to herself her country ruined, herself a captive, and her son dependent for his bread on the charity of strangers. When Achilles and the Greeks had taken their revenge on the killer of Patroclus they busied themselves in paying due funeral rites to their friend. A pile was erected, and the body burned with due solemnity; and then ensued games of strength and skill, chariot races, wrestling, boxing, and archery. Then the chiefs sat down to the funeral banquet and after that retired to rest. But Achilles neither partook of the feast nor of sleep. The recollection of his lost friend kept him awake, remembering their companionship in toil and dangers, in battle or on the perilous deep. Before the earliest dawn he left his tent, and joining to his chariot his swift steeds, he fastened Hector's body to be dragged behind. Twice he dragged him round the tomb of Patroclus, leaving him at length stretched in the dust. But Apollo would not permit the body to be torn or disfigured with all this abuse, but preserved it free from all taint or defilement. When Achilles indulged his wrath in thus disgracing brave Hector, Jupiter in pity summoned Thetis to his presence. He told her to go to her son and prevail on him to restore the body of Hector to his friends. Then Jupiter sent Iris to King Priam to encourage him to go to Achilles and beg the body of his son. Iris delivered her message, and Priam immediately prepared to obey. He opened his treasures and took out rich garments and cloths, with ten talents in gold and two splendid tripods and a golden cup of matchless workmanship. Then he called to his sons and bade them draw forth his litter and place in it the various articles designed for a ransom to Achilles. When all was ready, the old king with a single companion, as aged as himself, the herald Idaeus, drove forth from the gates, parting there with Hecuba his queen, and all his friends, who lamented him as going to certain death. But Jupiter, beholding with compassion the venerable king, sent Mercury to be his guide and protector. Mercury, assuming the form of a young warrior, presented himself to the aged couple, and while at the sight of him they hesitated whether to fly or yield, the god approached, and grasping Priam's hand, offered to be their guide to Achilles' tent. Priam gladly accepted his offered service, and he, mounting the carriage, assumed the reins and soon conveyed them to the tent of Achilles. Mercury's wand put to sleep all the guards, and without hindrance he introduced Priam into the tent where Achilles sat, attended by two of his warriors. The old king threw himself at the feet of Achilles and kissed those terrible hands that had destroyed so many of his sons. "Think, O Achilles," he said, "of thy own father, full of days like me, and trembling on the gloomy verge of life. Perhaps even now some neighbor chief oppresses him, and there is none at hand to succor him in his distress. Yet doubtless knowing that Achilles lives he still rejoices, hoping that one day he shall see thy face again. But no comfort cheers me, whose bravest sons, so late the flower of Ilium, all have fallen. Yet one I had, one more than all the rest the strength of my age, whom fighting for his country, thou hast slain. I come to redeem his body, bringing inestimable ransom with me. Achilles, reverence the gods! Recollect thy father! For his sake show compassion to me!" These words moved Achilles and he wept; remembering by turns his absent father and his lost friend. Moved with pity of Priam's silver locks and beard, he raised him from the earth and thus spake: "Priam, I know that thou has reached this place conducted by some god, for without divine aid no mortal even in the prime of youth had dared the attempt. I grant thy request; moved thereto by the evident will of Jove." So saying he arose, and went forth with his two friends, and unloaded of its charge the litter, leaving two mantles and a robe for the covering of the body, which they placed on the litter, and spread the garments over it, that not unveiled it should be borne back to Troy. Then Achilles dismissed the old king with his attendants, having first pledged himself to allow a truce of twelve days for the funeral solemnities. As the litter approached the city and was descried from the walls, the people poured forth to gaze once more on the face of their hero. Foremost of all, the mother and the wife of Hector came, and at the sight of the lifeless body renewed their lamentations. The people all wept with them, and to the going down of the sun there was no pause or abatement of their grief. The next day preparations were made for the funeral solemnities. For nine days the people brought wood and built the pile, and on the tenth they placed the body on the summit and applied the torch; while all Troy, thronging forth, encompassed the pile. When it had completely burned, they quenched the cinders with wine, collected the bones and placed them in a golden urn, which they buried in the earth, and reared a pile of stones over the spot. "Such honors Ilium to her hero paid, And peaceful slept the mighty Hector's shade."

CHAPTER XIX: THE FALL OF TROY. RETURN OF THE GREEKS. ORESTES AND ELECTRA.

The story of the Iliad ends with the death of Hector, and it is from the *Odyssey* and later poems that we learn the fate of the other heroes. After the death of Hector, Troy did not immediately fall, but receiving aid from new allies still continued its resistance. One of these allies was Memnon, whose story we have already told. Another was Penthesilea, queen of the Amazons, who came with a band of female warriors. All the authorities attest their valor and the fearful effect of their war cry. Penthesilea slew many of the bravest warriors, but was at last slain by Achilles. But when the hero bent over his fallen foe, and contemplated her beauty, youth and valor, he bitterly regretted his victory. Thersites, an insolent brawler and demagogue, ridiculed his grief, and was in consequence slain by the hero. Achilles by chance had seen Polyxena, daughter of King Priam, perhaps on occasion of the truce that was allowed the Trojans for the burial of Hector. He was captivated with her charms, and to win her in marriage agreed to use his influence with the Greeks to grant peace to Troy. While in the temple of Apollo, negotiating the marriage, Paris discharged at him a poisoned arrow, which guided by Apollo, wounded Achilles in the heel, the only vulnerable part about him. For Thetis, his mother, had dipped him when an infant in the river Styx, which made every part of him invulnerable except the heel by which she held him. The body of Achilles, so treacherously slain, was rescued by Ajax and Ulysses. Thetis directed the Greeks to bestow her son's armor on the hero who, of all survivors, should be judged most deserving of it. Ajax and Ulysses were the only claimants; a select number of the other chiefs were appointed to award the prize. It was awarded to Ulysses, thus placing wisdom before valor; whereupon Ajax slew himself. On the spot where his blood sank into the earth a flower sprang up, called the hyacinth, bearing on its leaves the first two letters of the name of Ajax, Ai, the Greek for "woe." Thus Ajax is a claimant with the boy Hyacinthus for the honor of giving birth to this flower. There is a species of larkspur that represents the hyacinth of the poets in preserving the memory of this event, the Delphinium Ajacis, Ajax's Larkspur.

It was now discovered that Troy could not be taken but by the arrows of Hercules. They were in possession of Philoctetes, the friend who had been with Hercules at the last, and lighted his funeral pyre. Philoctetes had joined the Grecian expedition against Troy, but had accidentally wounded his foot with one of the poisoned arrows, and the smell from his wound proved so offensive that his companions carried him to the Isle of Lemnos and left him there. Diomedes was now sent to induce him to rejoin the army. He succeeded. Philoctetes was cured of his wound by Machaon, and Paris was the first victim of the fatal arrows. In his distress Paris bethought him of one whom in his prosperity he had forgotten. This was the nymph Oenone, whom he had married when a youth, and had abandoned for the fatal beauty Helen. Oenone, remembering the wrongs she had suffered, refused to heal the wound, and Paris went back to Troy and died. She quickly repented and hastened after him with remedies, but came too late, and in her grief hung herself.

Fall of Troy, Unknown Italian painter, 17th century, oil on canvas

There was in Troy a celebrated statue of Minerva called the Palladium. It was said to have fallen from heaven, and the belief was that the city could not be taken so long as this statue remained within it. Ulysses and Diomedes entered the city in disguise, and succeeded in obtaining the Palladium, which they carried off to the Grecian camp. But Troy still held out, and the Greeks began to despair of ever subduing it by force, and by advice of Ulysses resolved to resort to stratagem. They pretended to be making preparations to abandon the siege, and a portion of the ships were withdrawn, and lay hid behind a neighboring island. The Greeks then constructed an immense wooden horse, which they gave out was intended as a propitiatory offering to Minerva, but in fact was filled with armed men. The remaining Greeks then betook themselves to their ships and sailed away, as if for a final departure. The Trojans, seeing the encampment broken up and the fleet gone, concluded the enemy to have abandoned the siege. The gates were thrown open, and the whole population issued forth rejoicing at the long prohibited liberty of passing freely over the scene of the late encampment. The great horse was the chief object of curiosity. All wondered what it could be for. Some recommended to take it into the city as a trophy; others felt afraid of it. While they hesitate, Laocoon, the priest of Neptune, exclaims, "What madness, citizens, is this! Have you not learned enough of Grecian fraud to be on your guard against it? For my part I fear the Greeks even when they offer gifts." So saying he threw his lance at the horse's side. It struck, and a hollow sound reverberated like a groan. Then perhaps the people might have taken his advice and destroyed the fatal horse and all its contents; but just at that moment a group of people appeared dragging forward one who seemed a prisoner and a Greek. Stupefied with terror he was brought before the chiefs, who reassured him, promising that his life should be spared on condition of his returning true answers to the questions asked him. He informed them that he was a Greek, Sinon by name, and that in consequence of the malice of Ulysses he had been left behind by his countrymen at their departure. With regard to the wooden horse, he told them that it was a propitiatory offering to Minerva and made so huge for the express purpose of preventing its being carried within the city; for Calchas the prophet had told them that if the Trojans took possession of it, they would assuredly triumph over the Greeks. This language turned the tide of the people's feelings, and they began to think how they might best secure the monstrous horse and the favorable auguries connected with it, when suddenly a prodigy occurred which left no room to doubt. There appeared advancing over the sea two immense serpents. They came upon the land, and the crowd fled in all directions. The serpents advanced directly to the spot where Laocoon stood with his two sons. They first attacked the children, winding round their bodies and breathing their pestilential breath in their faces. The father, attempting to rescue them, is next seized and involved in the serpents' coils. He struggles to tear them away, but they overpower all his efforts and strangle him and the children in their poisonous folds. This event was regarded as a clear indication of the displeasure of the gods at Laocoon's irreverent treatment of the wooden horse, which they no longer hesitated to regard as a sacred object and prepared to introduce with due solemnity into the city. This was done with songs and triumphal acclamations, and the day closed with festivity. In the night the armed men who were enclosed in the body of the horse, being led out by the traitor Sinon, opened the gates of the city to their friends who had returned under cover of the night. The city was set on fire; the people, overcome with feasting and sleep, put to the sword, and Troy completely subdued.

King Priam lived to see the downfall of his kingdom and was slain at last on the fatal night when the Greeks took the city. He had armed himself and was about to mingle with the combatants, but was prevailed on by Hecuba, his aged queen, to take refuge with herself and his daughters as a suppliant at the altar of Jupiter. While there, his youngest son Polites, pursued by Pyrrhus the son of Achilles, rushed in wounded, and expired at the feet of his father; whereupon Priam, overcome with indignation, hurled his spear with feeble hand against Pyrrhus and was forthwith slain by him. Queen Hecuba and her daughter Cassandra were carried captives to Greece. Cassandra had been loved by Apollo, and he gave her the gift of prophecy; but afterwards offended with her, he rendered the gift unavailing by ordaining that her predictions should never be believed. Polyxena, another daughter, who had been loved by Achilles, was demanded by the ghost of this warrior, and was sacrificed by the Greeks upon his tomb.

MENELAUS AND HELEN

Our readers will be anxious to know the fate of Helen, the fair but guilty occasion of so much slaughter. On the fall of Troy Menelaus recovered possession of his wife, who had not ceased to love him, though she had yielded to the might of Venus and deserted him for another. After the death of Paris she aided the Greeks secretly on several occasions, and in particular when Ulysses and Diomedes entered the city in disguise to carry off the Palladium. She saw and recognized Ulysses, but kept the secret and even assisted them in obtaining the image. Thus she became reconciled to her husband, and they were among the first to leave the shores of Troy for their native land. But having incurred the displeasure of the gods they were driven by storms from shore to shore of the Mediterranean, visiting Cyprus, Phoenicia and Egypt. In Egypt they were kindly treated and presented with rich gifts, of which Helen's share was a golden spindle and a basket on wheels. The basket was to hold the wool and spools for the queen's work. Menelaus and Helen at length arrived in safety at Sparta, resumed their royal dignity, and lived and reigned in splendor; and when Telemachus, the son of Ulysses, in search of his father, arrived at Sparta, he found Menelaus and Helen celebrating the marriage of their daughter Hermione to Neoptolemus, son of Achilles. In "the Victory Feast,"

AGAMEMNON, ORESTES, AND ELECTRA

Agamemnon, the general-in-chief of the Greeks, the brother of Menelaus, who had been drawn into the quarrel to avenge another's wrongs, was not so fortunate in the issue as his brother. During his absence his wife Clytemnestra had been false to him, and when his return was expected, she, with her paramour, Aegisthus, laid a plan for his destruction, and at the banquet given to celebrate his return, murdered him. The conspirators intended also to slay his son Orestes, a lad not yet old enough to be an object of apprehension, but from whom, if he should be suffered to grow up, there might be danger. Electra, the sister of Orestes, saved her brother's life by sending him secretly away to his uncle Strophius, king of Phocis. In the palace of Strophius, Orestes grew up with the king's son, Pylades and formed with him an ardent friendship. Electra frequently reminded her brother by messengers of the duty of avenging his father's death, and when grown up he consulted the oracle of Delphi, which confirmed him in his design. He therefore repaired in disguise to Argos, pretending to be a messenger from Strophius, who had come to announce the death of Orestes, and brought the ashes of the deceased in a funeral urn. After visiting his father's tomb and sacrificing upon it, according to the rites of the ancients, he made himself known to his sister Electra, and soon after slew both Aegisthus and Clytemnestra. This revolting act, the slaughter of a mother by her son, though alleviated by the guilt of the victim and the express command of the gods, did not fail to awaken in the breasts of the ancients the same abhorrence that it does in ours. The Eumenides, avenging deities, seized upon Orestes, and drove him frantic from land to land. Pylades accompanied him in his wanderings and watched over him. At length in answer to a second appeal to the oracle, he was directed to go to Tauris in Scythia, and to bring thence a statue of Diana, which was believed to have fallen from heaven. Accordingly Orestes and Pylades went to Tauris, where the barbarous people were accustomed to sacrifice to the goddess all strangers who fell into their hands. The two friends were seized and carried bound to the temple to be made victims. But the priestess of Diana was no other than Iphigenia, the sister of Orestes, who, our readers will remember, was snatched away by Diana, at the moment when she was about to be sacrificed. Ascertaining from the prisoners who they were, Iphigenia disclosed herself to them, and the three made their escape with the statue of the goddess, and returned to Mycenae. But Orestes was not yet relieved from the vengeance of the Erinnyes. At length he took refuge with Minerva at Athens. The goddess afforded him protection, and appointed the court of Areopagus to decide his fate. The Erinnyes brought forward their accusation, and Orestes made the command of

Orestes and Iphigenia, **2nd–3rd century,** BCE, **Mosaic, Musei Capitolini, Rome** (Photograph © Carole Raddato)

the Delphic oracle his excuse. When the court voted and the voices were equally divided, Orestes was acquitted by the command of Minerva.

One of the most moving scenes in the ancient drama is that in which Sophocles represents the meeting of Orestes and Electra, on his return from Phocis. Orestes, mistaking Electra for one of the domestics, and desirous of keeping his arrival a secret until the hour of vengeance should arrive, produces the urn in which his ashes are supposed to rest. Electra, believing him to be really dead, takes the urn, and embracing it, pours forth her grief in language full of tenderness and despair.

CHAPTER XX: THE ODYSSEY.

The romantic poem of the Odyssey is now to engage our attention. It narrates the wanderings of Ulysses (Odysseus in the Greek language) in his return from Troy to his own kingdom of Ithaca. From Troy the vessels first made land at Ismarus, a city of the Ciconians, where, in a skirmish with the inhabitants, Ulysses lost six men from each ship. Sailing thence they were overtaken by a storm that drove them for nine days along the sea until they reached the country of the Lotus-eaters. Here, after watering, Ulysses sent three of his men to discover who the inhabitants were. These men on coming among the Lotus-eaters were kindly entertained by them and were given some of their own food, the lotus-plant to eat. The effect of this food was such that those who partook of it lost all thoughts of home and wished to remain in that country. It was by main force that Ulysses dragged these men away, and he was even obliged to tie them under the benches of his ship.

They next arrived at the country of the Cyclopes. The Cyclopes were giants, who inhabited an island of which they were the only possessors. The name means "round eye," and these giants were so called because they had but one eye, and that placed in the middle of the forehead. They dwelt in caves and fed on the wild productions of the island and on what their flocks yielded, for they were shepherds. Ulysses left the main body of his ships at anchor, and with one vessel went to the Cyclopes' island to explore for supplies. He landed with his companions, carrying with them a jar of wine for a present, and coming to a large cave they entered it, and finding no one within examined its contents. They found it stored with the riches of the flock, quantities of cheese, pails and bowls of milk, lambs and kids in their pens, all in nice order. Presently arrived the master of the cave, Polyphemus, bearing an immense bundle of firewood, which he threw down before the cavern's mouth. He then drove into the cave the sheep and goats to be milked, and, entering, rolled to the cave's mouth an enormous rock, that twenty oxen could not draw. Next he sat down and milked his ewes, preparing a part for cheese, and setting the rest aside for his customary drink. Then turning round his great eye he discerned the strangers and growled out to them, demanding who they were, and where from. Ulysses replied most humbly, stating that they were Greeks, from the great expedition that had lately won so much glory in the conquest of Troy; that they were now on their way home and finished by imploring his hospitality in the name of the gods. Polyphemus deigned no answer, but reaching out his hand, seized two of the Greeks, whom he hurled against the side of the cave and dashed out their brains. He proceeded to devour them with great relish and having made a hearty meal, stretched himself out on the floor to sleep. Ulysses was tempted to seize the opportunity and plunge his sword into him as he slept, but recollected that it would only expose them all to certain destruction, as the rock with which the giant had closed up the door was far beyond their power to remove, and they would therefore be in hopeless imprisonment. Next morning the giant seized two more of the Greeks and dispatched them in the same manner as their companions, feasting on their flesh until no fragment was left. He then moved away the rock from the door, drove out his flocks, and went out, carefully replacing the barrier after him. When he was gone Ulysses planned how he might take vengeance for his murdered friends and effect his escape with his surviving companions. He made his men prepare a massive bar of wood cut by the Cyclops for a staff, which they found in the cave. They sharpened the end of it and seasoned it in the fire, and hid it under the straw on the cavern floor. Then four of the boldest were selected, with whom Ulysses joined himself as a fifth. The Cyclops came home at evening, rolled away the stone and drove in his flock as usual. After milking them and making his arrangements as before, he seized two more of Ulysses' companions and dashed their brains out, and made his evening meal upon them as he had on the others. After he had supped, Ulysses, approaching him, handed him a bowl of wine, saying, "Cyclops, this is wine; taste and drink after thy meal of man's flesh." He took and drank it, and was hugely delighted with it and called for more. Ulysses supplied him once and again, which pleased the giant so much that he promised him as a favor that he should be the last of the party devoured. He asked his name, to which Ulysses replied, "My name is Noman." After his supper the giant lay down to repose, and was soon sound asleep. Then Ulysses with his four select friends thrust the end of the stake into the fire until it was all one burning coal, then poising it exactly above the giant's only eye, they buried it deeply into the socket, twirling it round and round as a carpenter does his auger. The howling monster filled the cavern with his outcry, and Ulysses with his aids nimbly got out of his way and concealed themselves in the cave. The Cyclops, bellowing, called aloud on all the Cyclopes dwelling in the caves around him, far and near. They on his cry flocked around the den and inquired

John William Waterhouse, *Circe Invidiosa,* **1892 oil on canvas, Art Gallery of South Australia**

what grievous hurt had caused him to sound such an alarm and break their slumbers. He replied, "O friends, I die, and Noman gives the blow." They answered, "If no man hurts thee it is the stroke of Jove, and thou must bear it." So saying, they left him groaning. Next morning the Cyclops rolled away the stone to let his flock out to pasture but planted himself in the door of the cave to feel of all as they went out, that Ulysses and his men should not escape with them. But Ulysses had made his men harness the rams of the flock three abreast, with osiers, which they found on the floor of the cave. To the middle ram of the three one of the Greeks suspended himself, so protected by the exterior rams on either side. As they passed, the giant felt of the animals' backs and sides, but never thought of their bellies; so the men all passed safe, Ulysses himself being on the last one that passed. When they had got a few paces from the cavern, Ulysses and his friends released themselves from their rams, and drove a good part of the flock down to the shore to their boat. They put them aboard with all haste, then pushed off from the shore, and when at a safe distance Ulysses shouted, "Cyclops, the gods have well requited thee for thy atrocious deeds. Know it is Ulysses to whom thou owest thy shameful loss of sight." The Cyclops, hearing this, seized a rock that projected from the side of the mountain, and rending it from its bed he lifted it high in the air, then exerting all his force, hurled it in the direction of the voice. Down came the mass, just clearing the vessel's stern. The ocean, at the plunge of the huge rock, heaved the ship towards the land, so that it barely escaped being swamped by the waves. When they had with the utmost difficulty pulled off shore, Ulysses was about to hail the giant again, but his friends besought him not to do so. He could not forbear, however, letting the giant know that they had escaped his missile, but waited until they had reached a safer distance than before. The giant answered them with curses, but Ulysses and his friends plied their oars vigorously, and soon regained their companions.

Ulysses next arrived at the island of Aeolus. To this monarch Jupiter had entrusted the government of the winds, to send them forth or retain them at his will. He treated Ulysses hospitably, and at his departure gave him, tied up in a leathern bag with a silver string, such winds as might be hurtful and dangerous, commanding fair winds to blow the barks towards their country. Nine days they sped before the wind, and all that time Ulysses had stood at the helm, without sleep. At last quite exhausted he lay down to sleep. While he slept, the crew conferred together about the mysterious bag, and concluded it must contain treasures given by the hospitable King Aeolus to their commander. Tempted to secure some portion for themselves they loosed the string, when immediately the winds rushed forth. The ships were driven far from their course, and back again to the island they had just left. Aeolus was so indignant at their folly that he refused to assist them further, and they were obliged to labor over their course once more by means of their oars.

THE LAESTRYGONIANS

The next adventure was with the barbarous tribe of Laestrygonians. The vessels pushed into the harbor, tempted by the secure appearance of the cove, completely landlocked; Ulysses alone moored his vessel without. As soon as the Laestrygonians found the ships completely in their power they attacked them, having huge stones which broke and overturned them, and with their spears dispatched the seamen as they struggled in the water. All the vessels with their crews were destroyed, except Ulysses' own ship, which had remained outside, and finding no safety but in flight, he exhorted his men to ply their oars vigorously, and they escaped. With grief for their slain companions mixed with joy at their own escape, they pursued their way until they arrived at the Aeaean isle, where dwelt Circe, the daughter of the sun. Landing here Ulysses climbed a hill, and gazing round saw no signs of habitation except in one spot at the center of the island, where he perceived a palace embowered with trees. He sent forward one half of his crew, under the command of Eurylochus, to see what prospect of hospitality they might find. As they approached the palace, they found themselves surrounded by lions, tigers and wolves, not fierce, but tamed by Circe's art, for she was a powerful magician. All these animals had once been men, but had been changed by Circe's enchantments into the forms of beasts. The sounds of soft music were heard from within, and a sweet female voice singing. Eurylochus called aloud, and the goddess came forth and invited them in. They all gladly entered except Eurylochus, who suspected danger. The goddess instructed her guests to sit and had them served with wine and other delicacies. When they had feasted heartily, she touched them one by one with her wand, and they became immediately changed into swine, in "head, body, voice and bristles," yet with their intellects as before. She shut them in her sties, and supplied them with acorns and such other things as swine love. Eurylochus hurried back to the ship and told the tale. Ulysses thereupon determined to go himself and try if by any means he might deliver his companions. As he strode onward alone, he met a youth who addressed him familiarly, appearing to be acquainted with his adventures. He announced himself as Mercury and informed Ulysses of the arts of Circe, and of the danger of approaching her. As Ulysses was not to be dissuaded from his attempts, Mercury provided him with a sprig of the plant Moly, of wonderful power to resist sorceries and instructed him how to act. Ulysses proceeded and reaching the palace was courteously received by Circe, who entertained him as she had done his companions, and after he had eaten and drank, touched him with her wand, saying, "Hence seek the sty and wallow with thy friends." But he, instead of obeying, drew his sword and rushed upon her with fury in his countenance. She fell on her knees and begged for mercy. He dictated a solemn oath that she would release his companions and

practice no further against him or them; and she repeated it, at the same time promising to dismiss them all in safety after hospitably entertaining them. She was as good as her word. The men were restored to their shapes, the rest of the crew summoned from the shore, and the whole magnificently entertained day after day, until Ulysses seemed to have forgotten his native land, and to have reconciled himself to an inglorious life of ease and pleasure.

At length his companions recalled him to nobler sentiments, and he received their admonition gratefully. Circe aided their departure, and instructed them how to pass safely by the coast of the Sirens. The Sirens were sea nymphs who had the power of charming by their song all who had heard them, so that the unhappy mariners were irresistibly impelled to cast themselves into the sea to their destruction. Circe directed Ulysses to fill the ears of his seamen with wax, so that they should not hear the strain; and to cause himself to be bound to the mast, and his people to be strictly enjoined, whatever he might say or do, by no means to release him until they should have passed the Sirens' island. Ulysses obeyed these directions. He filled the ears of his people with wax, and suffered them to bind him with cords firmly to the mast. As they approached the Sirens' island, the sea was calm, and over the waters came the notes of music so ravishing and attractive, that Ulysses struggled to get loose, and by cries and signs to his people, begged to be released; but they, obedient to his previous orders, sprang forward and bound him still faster. They held on their course, and the music grew fainter until it ceased to be heard, when with joy Ulysses gave his companions the signal to unseal their ears, and they relieved him from his bonds.

SCYLLA AND CHARYBDIS

Ulysses had been warned by Circe of the two monsters Scylla and Charybdis. We have already met with

Scylla in the story of Glaucus, and remember that she was once a beautiful maiden and was changed into a snaky monster by Circe. She dwelt in a cave high up on the cliff, from whence she was accustomed to thrust forth her long necks for she had six heads, and in each of her mouths to seize one of the crew of every vessel passing within reach. The other terror, Charybdis, was a gulf, nearly on a level with the water. Thrice each day the water rushed into a frightful chasm, and thrice was disgorged. Any vessel coming near the whirlpool when the tide was rushing in must inevitably be engulfed; not Neptune himself could save it. On approaching the haunt of the dread monsters, Ulysses kept strict watch to discover them. The roar of the waters as Charybdis engulfed them, gave warning at a distance, but Scylla could nowhere be discerned. While Ulysses and his men watched with anxious eyes the dreadful whirlpool, they were not equally on their guard from the attack of Scylla, and the monster darting forth her snaky heads, caught six of his men, and bore them away shrieking to her den. It was the saddest sight Ulysses had yet seen; to behold his friends thus sacrificed and hear their cries, unable to afford them any assistance.

Circe had warned him of another danger. After passing Scylla and Charybdis, the next land he would make was Trinakria, an island whereon were pastured the cattle of Hyperion, the Sun, tended by his daughters Lampetia and Phaethusa. These flocks must not be violated, whatever the wants of the voyagers might be. If this injunction were transgressed, destruction was sure to fall on the offenders. Ulysses would willingly have passed the island of the Sun without stopping, but his companions so urgently pleaded for the rest and refreshment that would be derived from anchoring and passing the night on shore, that Ulysses yielded. He bound them, however, with an oath that they would not touch one of the animals of the sacred flocks and herds, but content themselves with what provision they yet had left of the supply that Circe had put on board. So long as this supply lasted the people kept their oath, but contrary winds detained them at the island for a month, and after consuming all their stock of provisions, they were forced to rely upon the birds and fishes they could catch. Famine pressed them, and at length one day, in the absence of Ulysses, they slew some of the cattle, vainly attempting to make amends for the deed by offering from them a portion to the offended powers. Ulysses, on his return to the shore, was horror struck at perceiving what they had done, and the more so on account of the portentous signs that followed. The skins crept on the ground, and the joints of meat lowed on the spits while roasting. The wind becoming fair they sailed from the island. They had not gone far when the weather changed, and a storm of thunder and lightning ensued. A stroke of lightning shattered their mast, which in its fall killed the pilot. At last the vessel itself came to pieces. The keel and mast floating side by side, Ulysses formed of them a raft, to which he clung, and, the wind changing, the waves bore him to Calypso's island. All the rest of the crew perished.

CALYPSO

Calypso was a sea-nymph. One of that numerous class of female divinities of lower rank than the gods yet sharing many of their attributes. Calypso received Ulysses hospitably, entertained him magnificently, became enamored of him, and wished to retain him forever, conferring on him immortality. But he persisted in his resolution to return to his country and his wife and son. Calypso at last received a command from Jove to dismiss him. Mercury brought the message to her, and found her in her grotto, which is thus described by Homer: "A garden vine, luxuriant on all sides, Mantled the spacious cavern, cluster-hung Profuse; four fountains of serenest lymph, Their sinuous course pursuing side by side, Strayed all around, and every where appeared Meadows of softest verdure purpled o'er With violets;

it was a scene to fill A god from heaven with wonder and delight." Calypso with much reluctance proceeded to obey the commands of Jupiter. She supplied Ulysses with the means of constructing a raft, provisioned it well for him, and gave him a favoring gale. He sped on his course prosperously for many days, until at length, when in sight of land, a storm arose that broke his mast, and threatened to rend the raft asunder. In this crisis he was seen by a compassionate sea-nymph, who in the form of a cormorant alighted on the raft, and presented him a girdle, directing him to bind it beneath his breast, and if he should be compelled to trust himself to the waves, it would buoy him up and enable him by swimming to reach the land.

TELEMACHUS

Telemachus was the son of Ulysses. Among other places at which he arrived, following on his father's footsteps, was Calypso's isle, and, as in the former case, the goddess tried every art to keep him with her and offered to share her immortality with him. But Minerva, who, in the shape of Mentor, accompanied him and governed all his movements, made him repel her allurements, and when no other means of escape could be found, the two friends leaped from a cliff into the sea, and swam to a vessel which lay becalmed off shore.

THE PHAEACIANS

Ulysses clung to the raft while any of its timbers kept together, and when it no longer yielded him support, binding the girdle around him, he swam. Minerva smoothed the billows before him and sent him a wind that rolled the waves towards the shore. The surf beat high on the rocks and seemed to forbid approach; but at length finding calm water at the mouth of a gentle stream, he landed, spent with toil, breathless and speechless and almost dead. After some time reviving, he kissed the soil, rejoicing, yet at a loss what course to take. At a short distance he perceived a wood, to which he turned his steps. There finding a covert sheltered by intermingling branches alike from the sun and the rain, he collected a pile of leaves and formed a bed, on which he stretched himself, and heaping the leaves over him, fell asleep. The land where he was thrown was Scheria, the country of the Phaeacians. These people dwelt originally near the Cyclopes; but being oppressed by that savage race, they migrated to the isle of Scheria, under the conduct of Nausithous their king. They were, the poet tells us, a people akin to the gods, who appeared manifestly and feasted among them when they offered sacrifices and did not conceal themselves from solitary wayfarers when they met them. They had abundance of wealth and lived in the enjoyment of it undisturbed by the alarms of war, for as they dwelt remote from gain-seeking man, no enemy ever approached their shores, and they did not even need to make use of bows and quivers. Their chief employment was navigation. Their ships, which went with the velocity of birds, were endued with intelligence; they knew every port and needed no pilot. Alcinous, the son of Nausithous, was now their king, a wise and just sovereign, beloved by his people. Now it happened that the very night on which Ulysses was cast ashore on the Phaeacian island, and while he lay sleeping on his bed of leaves, Nausicaa, the daughter of the king, had a dream sent by Minerva, reminding her that her wedding-day was not far distant, and that it would be but a prudent preparation for that event to have a general washing of the clothes of the family. This was no slight affair, for the fountains were at some distance and the garments must be carried thither. On awaking, the princess hastened to her parents to tell them what was on her mind; not alluding to her wedding-day, but finding other reasons equally good. Her father readily assented and ordered the grooms to furnish forth a wagon for the purpose. The clothes were put therein, and the queen mother placed in the wagon, likewise an abundant supply of food and wine. The princess took her seat and plied the lash, her attendant virgins following her on foot. Arrived

Salvator Rosa, *Odysseus and Nausicaa*, c. 1655, oil on canvas, Los Angeles County Museum of Art at the riverside they turned out the mules to graze, and unloading the carriage, bore the garments down to the water and working with cheerfulness and alacrity soon dispatched their labor. Then having spread the garments on the shore to dry, and having themselves bathed, they sat down to enjoy their meal; after which they rose and amused themselves with a game of ball, the princess singing to them while they played. But when they had refolded the apparel and were about to resume their way to the town, Minerva caused the ball thrown by the princess to fall into the water, whereat they all screamed, and Ulysses awaked at the sound. Now we must picture to ourselves Ulysses, a shipwrecked mariner, but just escaped from the waves, and utterly destitute of clothing, awaking and discovering that only a few bushes were interposed between him and a group of young maidens, whom, by their deportment and attire, he discovered to be not mere peasant girls, but of a higher class. Sadly needing help, how could he yet venture, naked as he was, to discover himself and make his wants known? It certainly was a case worthy of the interposition of his patron goddess Minerva, who never failed him at a crisis. Breaking off a leafy branch from a tree, he held it before him and stepped out from the thicket. The virgins, at sight of him, fled in all directions, Nausicaa alone excepted, for Minerva aided and endowed her with courage and discernment. Ulysses, standing respectfully aloof, told his sad case, and besought the fair object (whether queen or goddess he professed he knew not) for food and clothing. The princess replied courteously, promising present relief and her father's hospitality when he should become acquainted with the facts. She called back her scattered maidens, chiding their alarm and reminding them that the Phaeacians had no enemies to fear. This man, she told them, was an unhappy wanderer, whom it was a duty to cherish, for the poor and stranger are from Jove. She bade them bring food and clothing, for some of her brothers' garments were among the contents of the wagon. When this was done, and

Ulysses, retiring to a sheltered place, had washed his body free from the sea-foam, clothed and refreshed himself with food, Pallas dilated his form and diffused grace over his ample chest and manly brows. The princess, seeing him, was filled with admiration, and scrupled not to say to her damsels that she wished the gods would send her such a husband. To Ulysses she recommended that he should repair to the city, following herself and train so far as the way lay through the fields; but when they should approach the city she desired that he would no longer be seen in her company, for she feared the remarks that rude and vulgar people might make on seeing her return accompanied by such a gallant stranger; to avoid which she directed him to stop at a grove adjoining the city, in which were a farm and garden belonging to the king. After allowing time for the princess and her companions to reach the city, he was then to pursue his way thither and would be easily guided by any he might meet to the royal abode. Ulysses obeyed the directions, and in due time proceeded to the city, on approaching which he met a young woman bearing a pitcher forth for water. It was Minerva, who had assumed that form. Ulysses accosted her, and desired to be directed to the palace of Alcinous the king. The maiden replied respectfully, offering to be his guide; for the palace, she informed him, stood near her father's dwelling. Under the guidance of the goddess, and by her power enveloped in a cloud which shielded him from observation, Ulysses passed among the busy crowd, and with wonder observed their harbor, their ships, their forum (the resort of heroes), and their battlements, until they came to the palace, where the goddess, having first given him some information of the country, king, and people he was about to meet, left him.

Ulysses, before entering the courtyard of the palace, stood and surveyed the scene. Its splendor astonished him. Brazen walls stretched from the entrance to the interior house, of which the doors were gold, the door-

Gerard de Lairesse, *The Return of Ulysses to Ithaca,* c. 1719, oil on canvas, Staatsgalerie im Neuen Schloss, Zweiggalerie der Bayerischen Staatsgemäldesammlungen posts silver, the lintels silver ornamented with gold. On either side were figures of mastiffs wrought in gold and silver, standing in rows as if to guard the approach. Along the walls were seats spread through all their length with mantles of finest texture, the work of Phaeacian maidens. On these seats the princes sat and feasted, while golden statues of graceful youths held in their hands lighted torches, which shed radiance over the scene. Full fifty female menials served in household offices, some employed to grind the corn, others to wind off the purple wool or ply the loom. For the Phaeacian women as far exceeded all other women in household arts as the mariners of that country did the rest of mankind in the management of ships. Without the court a spacious garden lay, in which grew many a lofty tree, pomegranate, pear, apple, fig, and olive. Neither winter's cold nor summer's drought arrested their growth, but they flourished in constant succession, some budding while others were maturing. The vineyard was equally prolific. In one quarter you might see the vines, some in blossom, some loaded with ripe grapes, and in another observe the vintners treading the wine press. On the garden's borders flowers of every hue bloomed all the year round, arranged with neatest art. In the midst two fountains poured forth their waters, one flowing by artificial channels over all the garden, the other conducted through the courtyard of the palace, whence every citizen might draw his supplies. Ulysses stood gazing in admiration, unobserved, for the cloud that Minerva spread around him still shielded him. At length, having sufficiently observed the scene, he advanced with rapid step into the hall where the chiefs and senators were assembled, pouring libation to Mercury, whose worship followed the evening meal. Just then Minerva dissolved the cloud and disclosed him to the assembled chiefs. Advancing toward the queen, he knelt at her feet and implored her favor and assistance to enable him to return to his native country. Then withdrawing, he seated himself in the manner of suppliants, at the hearthside.

For a time none spoke. At last an aged statesman, addressing the king, said, "It is not fit that a stranger who asks our hospitality should be kept waiting in suppliant guise, none welcoming him. Let him therefore be led to a seat among us and supplied with food and wine." At these words the king rising gave his hand to Ulysses and led him to a seat, displacing thence his own son to make room for the stranger. Food and wine were set before him and he ate and refreshed himself. The king then dismissed his guests, notifying them that the next day he would call them to council to consider what had best be done for the stranger. When the guests had departed and Ulysses was left alone with the king and queen, the queen asked him who he was and whence he came, and (recognizing the clothes which he wore as those which her maidens and herself had made) from whom he received his garments. He told them of his residence in Calypso's isle and his departure thence; of the wreck of his raft, his escape by swimming, and of the relief afforded by the princess. The parents heard approvingly, and the king promised to furnish him a ship in which he might return to his own land. The next day the assembled chiefs confirmed the promise of the king. A bark was prepared and a crew of stout rowers selected, and all betook themselves to the palace, where a bounteous repast was provided. After the feast the king proposed that the young men should show their guest their proficiency in manly sports, and all went forth to the arena for games of running, wrestling, and other exercises. After all had done their best, Ulysses being challenged to show what he could do, at first declined, but being taunted by one of the youths, seized a quoit of weight far heavier than any the Phaeacians had thrown, and sent it farther than the utmost throw of theirs. All were astonished, and viewed their guest with greatly increased respect.

After the games they returned to the hall, and the herald led in Demodocus, the blind bard, "Dear to the

Muse, Who yet appointed him both good and ill, Took from him sight, but gave him strains divine." He took for his theme the wooden horse, by means of which the Greeks found entrance into Troy. Apollo inspired him, and he sang so feelingly of the terrors and the exploits of that eventful time that all were delighted, but Ulysses was moved to tears. Observing which, Alcinous, when the song was done, demanded of him why at the mention of Troy his sorrows awaked. Had he lost there a father or brother, or any dear friend? Ulysses in reply announced himself by his true name, and at their request, recounted the adventures that had befallen him since his departure from Troy. This narrative raised the sympathy and admiration of the Phaeacians for their guest to the highest pitch. The king proposed that each chief should present him with a gift, himself setting the example. They obeyed, and vied with one another in loading the illustrious stranger with costly gifts. The next day Ulysses set sail in the Phaeacian vessel, and in a short time arrived safe at Ithaca, his own island.

When the vessel touched the strand he was asleep. The mariners, without waking him, carried him on shore, and landed with him the chest containing his presents, and then sailed away. But Neptune was displeased at the conduct of the Phaeacians in thus rescuing Ulysses from his hands. In revenge, on the return of the vessel to port, he transformed it into a rock, right opposite the mouth of the harbor.

FATE OF THE SUITORS

It was now twenty years that Ulysses had been away from Ithaca, and when he awoke he did not recognize his native land. But Minerva, appearing to him in the form of a young shepherd, informed him where he was and told him the state of things at his palace. More than a hundred nobles of Ithaca and of the neighboring islands had been for years suing for the hand of Penelope, his wife, imagining him dead, and lording it over his palace and people, as if they were owners of both. That he might be able to take vengeance upon them, it was important that he should not be recognized. Minerva accordingly metamorphosed him into an unsightly beggar, and as such he was kindly received by Eumaeus, the swineherd, a faithful servant of his house. Telemachus, his son, was absent in quest of his father. He had gone to the courts of the other kings, who had returned from the Trojan expedition. While on the search, he received counsel from Minerva to return home. Arriving at Ithaca, he sought Eumaeus to learn something of the state of affairs at the palace before presenting himself among the suitors. Finding a stranger with Eumaeus, he treated him courteously, though in the garb of a beggar, and promised him assistance. Eumaeus was sent to the palace to inform Penelope privately of her son's arrival, for caution was necessary with regard to the suitors, who, as Telemachus had learned, were plotting to intercept and kill him. When Eumaeus was gone, Minerva presented herself to Ulysses and directed him to make himself known to his son. At the same time she touched him, removed at once from him the appearance of age and penury and gave him the aspect of vigorous manhood that belonged to him. Telemachus viewed him with astonishment and at first thought he must be more than mortal. But Ulysses announced himself as his father, and accounted for the change of appearance by explaining that it was Minerva's doing.

Then threw Telemachus
His arms around his father's neck and wept,
Desire intense of lamentation seized
On both; soft murmurs uttering, each indulged
His grief.

The father and son took counsel together how they should get the better of the suitors and punish them for their outrages. It was arranged that Telemachus should

135

Thomas Degeorge, *Ulysses and Telemachus Massacring Penelope's Suitors,* 1812, Clermont-Ferrard Museum of Art (Photograph © VladounidoOo)

proceed to the palace and mingle with the suitors as formerly; that Ulysses should go also, as a beggar. Ulysses charged his son not to betray, by any display of unusual interest in him, that he knew him to be other than he seemed and, even if he saw him insulted or beaten, not to interpose otherwise than he might do for any stranger. At the palace they found the usual scene of feasting and riot going on. The suitors pretended to receive Telemachus with joy at his return, though secretly mortified at the failure of their plots to take his life. The old beggar was permitted to enter and provided with a portion from the table. A touching incident occurred as Ulysses entered the courtyard of the palace. An old dog lay in the yard almost dead with age, and seeing a stranger enter, raised his head, with ears erect. It was Argus, Ulysses' own dog that he had in other days often led to the chase.

> "Soon he perceived
> Long-lost Ulysses nigh, down fell his ears
> Clapped close, and with his tail glad signs he gave
> Of gratulation, impotent to rise,
> And to approach his master as of old.
> Ulysses, noting him, wiped off a tear
> Unmarked. . . .
> Then his destiny released
> Old Argus, soon as he had lived to see
> Ulysses in the twentieth year restored."

As Ulysses sat eating his portion in the hall, the suitors soon began to exhibit their insolence to him. When he mildly remonstrated, one of them raised a stool and with it gave him a blow. Telemachus had hard work to restrain his indignation at seeing his father so treated in his own hall, but remembering his father's injunctions, said no more than what became him as master of the house and protector of his guests. Penelope had protracted her decision in favor of any one of her suitors so long, that there seemed to be no further pre-

tense for delay. The continued absence of her husband seemed to prove that his return was no longer to be expected. Meanwhile her son had grown up, and was able to manage his own affairs. She therefore consented to submit the question of her choice to a trial of skill among the suitors. The test selected was shooting with the bow. Twelve rings were arranged in a line, and he whose arrow was sent through the whole twelve was to have the queen for his prize. A bow that one of his brother heroes had given to Ulysses in former times, was brought from the armory and with its quiver full of arrows was laid in the hall. Telemachus had taken care that all other weapons should be removed, under pretense that in the heat of competition, there was danger, in some rash moment, of putting them to an improper use. All things being prepared for the trial, the first thing to be done was to bend the bow in order to attach the string. Telemachus endeavored to do it but found all his efforts fruitless; and modestly confessing that he had attempted a task beyond his strength, he yielded the bow to another. He tried it with no better success, and, amidst the laughter and jeers of his companions, gave it up. Another tried it and another; they rubbed the bow with tallow, but all to no purpose; it would not bend. Then spoke Ulysses, humbly suggesting that he should be permitted to try; for, said he, "Beggar as I am, I was once a soldier, and there is still some strength in these old limbs of mine." The suitors hooted with derision and commanded to turn him out of the hall for his insolence. But Telemachus spoke up for him, and merely to gratify the old man, bade him try. Ulysses took the bow, and handled it with the hand of a master. With ease he adjusted the cord to its notch, then fitting an arrow to the bow he drew the string and sped the arrow unerring through the rings. Without allowing them time to express their astonishment, he said, "Now for another mark!" and aimed direct at the most insolent one of the suitors. The arrow pierced through his throat and he fell dead. Telemachus, Eumaeus, and another faithful follower, well armed, now sprang to the side of Ulysses. The suitors, in amazement, looked round for arms but found none, neither was there any way of escape, for Eumaeus had secured the door. Ulysses left them not long in uncertainty; he announced himself as the long-lost chief, whose house they had invaded, whose substance they had squandered, whose wife and son they had persecuted for ten long years; and told them he meant to have ample vengeance. All the suitors were slain, except Phemius the bard and Medon the herald, and Ulysses was left master of his own palace and possessor of his kingdom and his wife.